The Divine Source
and
World Unity

Selected Works of Adolph Moses for the 21st Century

The Divine Source
and
World Unity

Selected Works of Adolph Moses for the 21st Century

Compiled and Edited
by
William F. Shannon

Hudson Mohawk Press
Troy, NY

Hudson Mohawk Press LLC
400 Broadway #1726
Troy, New York 12180

www.hudsonmohawkpress.com
www.facebook.com/hudsonmohawkpress

This edited compilation published by Hudson Mohawk Press in January
2011. Chapters 1 through 6 were originally published in different form in
the collection entitled *Yahvism and Other Discourses*, published by The
Louisville Section of the Council of Jewish Women in 1903 in Louisville,
Kentucky.

ISBN 978-0-9843040-4-2 (paperback)

Library of Congress Control Number: 2011900097

Editing and book design by William F. Shannon

Printed in the United States

CONTENTS

INTRODUCTION

William F. Shannon

Adolph Moses (1840-1902) was born in Poland,
arrived in the United States in 1870, and was rabbi of
congregations in Alabama and Kentucky. He
identified with the more radical wing of American
Reform Judaism and was an anti-Zionist. As Oscar
Handlin put it, "Americans tended to be extremists in
the world Zionist movement, in no small measure
because they carried into it the whole burden of their
worries and fears as American Jews."[*] Adolph Moses
recognized this, and for him Zionism was at best a
folly and at worst the ultimate danger to Jews around
the world. He averred that the true religion of Moses
is recognition of the one God for everyone everywhere,
not a tribal religion forming the basis for a country in
the Middle East for a particular group of people.

Thus Moses emphasized the universal nature of
Judaism and all true religion. He scrutinized the
essence of his religion and adopted the term

---

[*] Oscar Handlin. *Adventure in Freedom: Three Hundred Years of
Jewish Live in America.* New York: McGraw-Hill, 1954, p. 217.

"Yahvism" to emphasize his conviction that Judaism was neither a national nor a tribal religion. He wanted to attract non-Jews to Judaism, and he wanted to lure back Jews who had lost affection for their religion. Most of all he wanted to show that Judaism is a religion for all those who are interested in learning about it, and *not* a religion exclusively or even primarily for those born as Jews. His vision was a new Church of Humanity grounded in the universal vision of the biblical prophets and based on the mutual respect, union and universal love of those who had formerly identified themselves as Jews or adherents of other religions.

His ideas represent an elegant effort to normalize and perpetuate the religion of Moses in the modern world. It is with his universal vision in mind that we present this selection of his writings in gender-neutral language, in recognition of Moses's desire to be a light to all people.

* * * * *

The remainder of this introduction combines a revision of text drawn from Hyman Gerson Enelow's 1903 introduction to "Yahvism and Other Discourses", rendered into gender-neutral language, with new text by the editor.

Adolph Moses taught the universal Truth of all religions. This Truth is a message about God in the world that goes beyond the specific language of any particular theology. As Professor Laura Ellen Shulman of Northern Virginia Community College puts it, "Whether a Jew refers to "Shekhinah", or a Christian to "Holy Spirit", or a Hindu to "Atman", or a

Buddhist to the "Buddha Nature" ... all faiths, all humans in all times and places, have sensed the immediate presence of "the One" among and amidst the many and in the heart and soul of each of us. God is so great as to have revealed Himself (sic) to all of us. Every religion of humanity is the inheritance of every individual human being ... Religious unity is found in that which is before and beyond all labels and appearances, in that which is the basis of all religions -- in God alone (whatever we may call it)."[†]

Moses's conception of Judaism was broad, shaking off the shackles of ceremonialism and racial exclusiveness. His Jewish faith was sufficiently broad to welcome *all people* and house *all* knowledge. He espoused a very lofty religious idealism that drew vitality from the remote founts of metaphysic thought, comfortably in line with the ideas of the New Thought philosophy prevalent in America at the turn of the 20th century. To Adolph Moses Judaism was not the religion of any one race or chosen people; it was *not* designed as the peculiar property of a particular set of people bound together by physical kinship. He deprecated most strenuously such "physiological Judaism". For him, the Torah was given in the wilderness, belonging to *all* people alike, so that everybody might come and claim an equal share in it. The quintessence of the ancient faith was the supreme doctrine of truth and morality, based on the belief in the one only God, founded by Moses, developed by the prophets, enriched by the thoughts and the divine ideals of *all* wise and noble people, witnessed by all the martyrs to Truth, and destined at some golden day

---

[†] http://www.nvcc.edu/home/lshulman/WHYIF.html

to unite all human hearts and minds by the sacred ties of righteousness and love.

He regarded the name "Judaism" as a misnomer and misfortune. Its origin, he contended, was exotic; it was fabricated as a countermark to Hellenism by Josephus, a man who tried to bow to the Western world, just as the ambitious Lord Beaconsfield, under somewhat similar circumstances, became the originator of modern Jewish racialism, of "the physiological Judaism," the Judaism of noble ancestry, of blue blood, fit to stand side by side, in point of pedigree, with Anglo-Saxon aristocracy. The name "Judaism", Moses argues further, has grown associated in the minds of people with a narrow racial creed, with the particular soul-business of some real or fictitious Hebrews, Semites, nay, with a complicated system of effete, oriental ceremonies and outlandish practices. And such certainly was not the nature of the doctrine the prophets taught, of the old world-wide religion founded on the unity of God, Nature, and Humanity. Yahweh, the God of the prophets, from wherever the name may have been borrowed, to the enlightened minds of Israel had come to designate the Creator of the world, the Parent of humanity, the Sovereign of nature, the Source ever-living of Justice, Righteousness, Truth, and Love. The service of Yahweh must embrace belief in the unity of the world, the furtherance of the commonwealth of humanity, the sacred quest of Truth, and unswerving loyalty to the cause of Righteousness. "Whom have I in heaven, but Thee? And there is none upon earth that I desire beside Thee," as the Psalmist has sung.

In this absolute subjection of the whole universe, of all life, of Humanity and Nature, to one only God, to Yahweh, lay the spiritual majesty of the Religion of

Yahweh, or what Adolph Moses dubbed "Yahvism". This differentiated it from paganism, which was inclined to parcel up humanity and the universe among a host of wrangling deities, and this has distinguished Yahvism from every other faith that in any manner whatever has tampered with the idea of the Divine Unity. Not that these other creeds had had no mission: on the contrary, every system of religious thought has had in its bosom a sacred germ of truth; "there is no break in the development of the spirit of humanity"; "God has left none of God's children without a ray of God's light." But all other faiths, in Moses's judgment, have been merely preparatory to the one universal creed which regards all people as family, all nature as the work of one Creator, and the whole cosmos as the servant of one dominant law of Righteousness; all other religions are mere broken arcs of idealism in relation to the one perfect round of Yahvism which encircles the whole throbbing, striving, yearning heart of the world.

The change in title to "Yahvism" would connote the true universal character of the religion; it would be mistaken no longer for the peculiar creed of a dispersed tribe from the Levant; it would cease to be the weapon of vicious anti-Semitic bigots, on the one hand, and ignorant, race-proud Jews, on the other; it would be rescued from the misuse of sentimental venerators of antiquated superstition and of the idolaters of obsolete ceremonies; it would arise before the world in its true nature, as the light of nations, as the reflection of the universal Spirit, as the principle of unity in the world and humanity, as the rule of righteousness and love amongst all people, as the knot of all culture, truths, and ideals; and it would draw to its bosom many a person who, though quite in accord with its sublime aims and tenets, now shrinks from its embrace by reason of old erroneous associations. The preaching of this idea, the advocacy of an inclusive, universal "Yahvism" was the distinctive contribution of Adolph Moses to the commonwealth of humanity. Poetry, philosophy, science, art, nature – the spirit of Yahweh moved upon the face of all.

Adolph Moses regarded America as the Promised Land of his cherished religion. It is in the United States, he held, that the follower of Yahweh had gained the unhampered opportunity of diffusing the doctrines of genuine Judaism, or Yahvism. He felt the old Jewish ceremonies served a good end in their proper age, but in the contemporary world they are nothing so much as the illegitimate encroachment of the past upon the territory of the present and the future. New circumstances have robbed them of the spirit of life; they linger on in our midst in the anemic manner of the shadows moving through Sheol. All attempts to revive them must fail; why babble about a return to rites and ceremonies which we have outgrown, why seek to raise up artificially things that are dead, to wheedle ourselves into obsolete beliefs which can no longer stir our breasts or better our souls? Dr. Moses was opposed—as a man holding his views of Judaism could not help being—to the schemes of the political Zionists, as well as to the nebulous movement of the New Orthodoxy with all its oracular watchwords relating to the past, historic continuity, the claims of the ancient literature, and suchlike. He knew that watchwords and romantic phrases and the kickshaws of theorists were not synonymous with life, that they would never respond to the vital needs and the spiritual yearnings of people living in the heart of American civilization. None revered the past and its sanctities more than he, but he believed that "religion," in the words of Robertson Smith, "can not live on the mere memory of the past."

Yahvism was advocated as the revival of an old term for an ancient truth, as a tie that possibly would unite people of similar thoughts and ideals now separated by the ill-luck of mutually exclusive labels, as a title that might serve to reconcile the highest forms of Judaism and Christianity and Islam. On the other hand, the essay, "Why I Am a Jew," shows that Moses did not turn his back upon Jews and Judaism, even in name, as long as a single human being, however humble and distant, were caused to suffer by reason of loyalty to the faith of Israel. It is here that we see in juxtaposition the diverse dominant elements of his character: the frankness of the unbiased scholar and the fervor of the universal idealist combined with an inexpugnable fidelity to the cause of his co-religionists.

At the bottom of all his thoughts and meditations lay a blend of Rationalism and Mysticism, a combination of Emotion and Reason, which formed the faith of the Prophets and the Psalmists, of Jeremiah and of Job, and which – who knows – may come to form the faith of the world. The day for the realization of the ideals of Adolph Moses has not yet arrived, and some would say that given the state of the world in the early 21st century is it farther away than ever, but let us hope that the selections of his work gathered in this book will help to bring the good day closer.

* * * *

WILLIAM F. SHANNON is the Publisher and Editor of Hudson Mohawk Press. He holds a Master of Arts in Integrated Studies/Cultural Studies from Athabasca University in Canada.

1885 DECLARATION OF PRINCIPLES
also known as
"THE 1885 PITTSBURGH PLATFORM"

Editor's Note

In November 1885, fifteen rabbis met in Pittsburgh, Pennsylvania, and adopted a declaration of principles that became the foundation of Reform Judaism in the United States; it would come to be known as the "1885 Pittsburgh Platform". Later convocations of Reform rabbis would undo many of these principles in later declarations, resulting in the much less universalistic interpretations of Reform Judaism that are more common in the United States today. The 1885 Declaration of Principles is a powerful example of how to interpret ancient religious truths in a modern context, a mode of religious thinking all too rare at the dawn of the 21st century in all religious traditions. The 1885 principles emphasize the universal commonwealth of all humanity, the kinship of Judaism with Christianity and Islam, and the Truth that can be found in all religions. These principles are behind the ideas presented by Adolph Moses in the essays to follow. The 1885 Declaration of Principles remains to this day the basis of the movement called "Classical Reform Judaism", a movement that does not receive as much attention in *mainstream media as do other interpretations of the religion of Moses. We present this document in the universalistic spirit in which it was drawn at the dawn of 20th century, when thoughtful people of all religious traditions were more concerned with elucidating what we all have in common as human beings, instead of emphasizing what might separate us, a valuable lesson from which we all could benefit in the 21st century.*

Text in brackets [ ] represents text rendered into gender-neutral language in recognition of the universalistic spirit of the 19th century document.

* * * * *

The 1885 Declaration of Principles

We recognize in every religion an attempt to grasp the Infinite, and in every mode, source or book of revelation, held sacred by any religious system, the consciousness of the indwelling of God in [each person]. We hold that Judaism presents the highest conception of the God-idea as taught in our Holy Scriptures and developed and spiritualized by the Jewish teachers, in accordance with the moral and philosophical progress of their respective ages. We maintain that Judaism preserved and defended, midst continual struggles and trials and under enforced isolation, this God-idea as the central religious truth for the human race.

We recognize in the Bible the record of the consecration of the Jewish people to its mission as priest of the one God, and value it as the most potent instrument of religious and moral instruction. We hold that the modern discoveries of scientific researches in the domains of nature and history are not antagonistic to the doctrines of Judaism, the Bible reflecting the primitive ideas of its own age, and at times clothing its conception of Divine Providence and justice dealing with [humanity] in miraculous narratives.

We recognize in the Mosaic legislation a system of training the Jewish people for its mission during its national life in Palestine, and today we accept as binding only the moral laws, and maintain only such ceremonies as elevate and sanctify our lives, but reject all such as are not adapted to the views and habits of modern civilization.

We hold that all such Mosaic and rabbinical laws as regulate diet, priestly purity and dress originated in ages and under influences of ideas altogether foreign to our present mental and spiritual state. They fail to impress the modern Jew with a spirit of holiness; their observance in our days is apt rather to obstruct than to further modern spiritual elevation.

We recognize in the modern era of universal culture of heart and intellect the approaching of the realization of Israel's great Messianic hope for the establishment of the kingdom of truth, justice and peace among all [people]. We consider ourselves no longer a nation, but a religious community, and, therefore, expect neither a return to Palestine, nor a sacrificial worship under the sons of Aaron, nor the restoration of any laws concerning the Jewish state.

We recognize in Judaism a progressive religion, ever striving to be in accord with the postulates of reason.

We are convinced of the utmost necessity of preserving the historical identity with our great past. Christianity and Islam being daughter religions of Judaism, we appreciate their providential mission to aid in the spreading of monotheistic and moral truth. We acknowledge that the spirit of broad humanity of our age is our ally in the fulfillment of our mission, and, therefore we extend the hand of fellowship to all who cooperate with us in the establishment of the reign of truth and righteousness among [all people].

We reassert the doctrine of Judaism that the soul of [each person] is immortal, grounding this belief on the divine nature of the human spirit, which forever finds bliss in righteousness and misery in wickedness. We reject, as ideas not rooted in Judaism, the beliefs both in bodily resurrection and in Gehenna and Eden (Hell and Paradise) as abodes for everlasting punishment and reward.

In full accordance with the spirit of Mosaic legislation, which strives to regulate the relation between rich and poor, we deem it our duty to participate in the great task of modern times, to solve, on the basis of justice and righteousness, the problems presented by the contrasts and evils of the present organization of society.

CHAPTER 1

The Religion We Offer to the Gentiles

Introductory

For the first time since the final triumph of Christianity over Paganism, for the first time since the victorious daughter-church had on pain of death forbidden the Jews to make converts, Yahvism, usually called Judaism, is in our time and country[‡] given a fair chance to renew its long interrupted propaganda, to make the attempt at gathering into the fold of our church those Gentiles whose heart and mind are out of harmony with the teachings of Christianity. The only one God, the Maker of heaven and earth, who spoke by the mouth of the prophets and revealed itself as the God and Parent, the Law-giver, Judge, and Guide of all humanity, is calling us by name, and bidding us to

---

[‡] The author is writing at the end of the 19th century in the United States.

1

gird our loins with strength, to bring to all the message of Yahvism, the message of God's all-embracing and all-quickening unity, the message of God's revealed laws of universal justice, the message of humanity to be redeemed by love and reconciled by entertaining the covenant of righteousness with God. A new time has begun and new work must be done by us. The God of history is putting to us, the children of this generation, a glorious task which is of infinite importance but also of infinite difficulty. Somewhere the beginning must be made by believing hearts and dauntless spirits. Those who are determined to walk in the path carved out by the inspired messengers of God must take the first bold steps toward assimilation by spiritual conquest — if not immediately in practice, at least in clearly-conceived theory. The time has come for us firmly to grasp the problem of our missionary calling. If God has foreordained us to be teachers, we should know what we are to teach: what cardinal principles of belief, what ideas of morality, what ideals of private and social conduct constitute the religion which we are to offer to people who do not call themselves by the name of Israel.

But many of those within the reach of our voice, and many more who will read this discourse, will smile at the high-aspiring claims which we make for the destiny of Yahvism. They will call our belief in the conquering future of our religion a pleasant day-dream which is at variance with the stubborn realities of the conditions given by history. "It is not thinkable," they will say, "that Yahvism will ever spread beyond the narrow limits of the Jewish race. Any such attempt is foredoomed to ignominious failure. It is not credible that the Jews will ever make propaganda for their religion. They do not show the least desire for such an adventurous and arduous mission. In their heart of hearts they firmly believe that Judaism is synonymous with the Jewish race. To them no less than to the Gentiles, it seems simply ridiculous that any but a born Jew should profess the religion of the Jews and be a member of the church of Yahweh."

To the doubters and the cavillers among my co-religionists I reply: If the Israelites have no wish to make propaganda for their faith, the worse for them, and the worse still for their descendants. Our present position in the world is a most dangerous anomaly. History furnishes no parallel to it. Nothing like it can be traced in the annals of the past, nothing corresponding to it can be found in the present on the whole face of the earth. We live scattered everywhere among the nations of the earth, we are distinguished by them and distinguishable from them. We are regarded as a distinct people, and many Jews, smitten with judicial blindness, accept this false and fatal view, and speak of themselves as belonging to the Jewish people. If we are indeed a separate nation or people, we have no business and no right to dwell in every part of the world, and to claim everywhere the privileges of full citizenship. We should as quickly as possible try to have a country, a language, and a government of our own, and thus constitute a nation in reality instead of being satisfied with being one in theory. There is consistency and method in the madness of the Zionists. They argue: "We have these many centuries been a nation living in exile. In former days it was impossible for us to return to our Land. Let us return as soon as possible to Palestine, occupy and till its soil like our forebears, revive our Hebrew language and make it our living national tongue, establish a government of our own, and once more play the part of a nation with our national religion for its basis." You laugh at this phantasmagoria of the Zionists, and consider it a most mischievous folly, little short of treason and blasphemy. For they are putting dangerous weapons in the hands of our enemies and maligners, who declare that the Jews are but interlopers, who ought to be deprived of the rights and prerogatives of citizenship and in every respect treated as aliens living in the land on sufferance, by the grace of the nation.

Let us not hide from ourselves the fact that the spirit of nationality has in this century become more intense, more self-conscious, and more intolerant than it ever was since the days of the Roman Empire. Nationality and race, for good, but more for evil, have come to be in our day the vital principles of every leading European state. They are the crystallizing forces of all new political formations in Europe. Community of race is declared to be the only natural and solid foundation of every commonwealth. The tremendous forces of nationality are rapidly disintegrating great empires such as Turkey and Austria, which are composed of different races and nations. Racial affinities are recognized as the only power of national cohesion. They alone are held to give to a state a reason and a right for existence. In former ages the ruling family or dynasty, in some cases religion, formed the bond of union between the component parts of a state. Most states, therefore, consisted of populations differing in race, language, manners, and customs. The idea of nationality and race, so strong in antiquity, was feebly developed in the Middle Ages, and played only an insignificant part in the political schemes of the rulers and the sympathies and antipathies of the masses. The reason is not far to seek. The modern nations themselves are of comparatively recent growth. They were very long in the making. They were slowly compounded and recompounded of numerous fragments of races and states. The very fact that the medieval emperor was the head of the Holy Roman Empire, which comprised all Germany, parts of France, Italy, Holland, Switzerland, Austria, Hungary, and Poland, clearly proves how undeveloped the idea of nationality was in medieval times and that it played at best but a secondary part in the political and social life of Europe. While the European nations were slowly evolving, religion was the principal force that united or separated individuals and kingdoms. In those days the Jews were deprived of human rights and cruelly persecuted in the name of religion. There was no racial, no national antipathy against them. In the nineteenth century the slow process of nation-making has been well-nigh completed in Europe. Nationality and race have been substituted for religion as the dominant principle of unity and separation among people. The fanaticism of religion has given place to the fanaticism of nationality. It has come to stay for a long time. It will for centuries to come direct the course of history, fashion the feelings and determine the acts of people in their individual and collective capacity.

The principle of nationality, the fanaticism of race, has within the last twenty-five years (*Editor's Note: Moses is referring to the last quarter of the 19th century (approx 1875-1900)*) risen in Europe against the Jews. Anti-Semitism is but the brutal and wicked expression of a most potent force with which we must reckon. Rightly or wrongly the continental nations believe that the Jews are an alien people, and as such are a foreign element in the body politic. The struggle is fierce and disgraceful, the antagonism full of perplexities and dangers. In a pamphlet recently published in Germany, a celebrated Jewish lawyer recommends assimilation in all things save religion as the only solution. His arguments have made a profound impression on many thinking people in Europe. There are far-sighted people in Europe and in America who love the cause of Israel better than their own life, who feel infinite love and pity for bruised and tormented Israel, for Israel the scapegoat of the nations. These men, with hearts full of sleepless sorrow, have come to recognize it as the will of God that Israel should, in the course of time, become a universal religion and church, instead of being an isolated race. Still, in Europe the conditions are less favorable to such a consummation. There is too much narrowness and prejudice on both sides. Israel's new light of salvation must and will come from America. Judaism or Yahvism will start on a new career of spiritual and moral conquest in America. Here, in this land of absolute religious liberty and endless possibilities, the faith of Israel is destined to shake off all trammels of race and become in all its activities and aspirations a universal religion, such as it has always been in essence and scope. The historical conditions surrounding us in this country are indefinitely more propitious to the evolution of Israel and Yahvism into the church of humanity. The spirit of nationality fortunately has not yet been developed in America to that degree of intensity and intolerance which has caused it to become in Europe in many respects hostile to the spirit of broad humanity. The American nation is in a large measure still in the making. Races physically and mentally the most varied are still dwelling peacefully together. The component parts have not yet been fused into a compact national unity, and new foreign elements are being constantly added to the variegated mass. But a time will come when the American nation will be completely formed, when all the heterogeneous elements will be transformed into an homogeneous people occupying in dense numbers the fruitful American land. Then the national spirit will become as strong and intolerant here as it already is in the Old World. The bars will be raised against foreign immigration. In theory and practice the rule will prevail, "America for the Americans." Then the fanaticism of nationality will be as virulent, as suspicious, and dangerous as it is today in Europe. The Know-nothing movement was but a premature prelude of what will come to be in fifty or a hundred years.

Let us bestir ourselves during these years, before the storms will burst upon us. Assimilation by making spiritual conquests, safety by enlarging and transforming into a universal Church, is the advice which far-seeing wisdom gives us. Our religion is dearer to us than life itself. We would rather be the outcasts of the world than become faithless to our faith. But this very religion of ours demands that we should preach its simple and broad truths to the nations. It is our mission to be a blessing to all the families of the earth. It is our calling to teach the absolute unity of God in opposition to all pagan adulterations of the faith of the prophets. It is our office to join unto ourselves all those who are our family in faith, though strangers in blood. The harvest to be gathered is rich, it requires infinite patience, enthusiasm, faith, endless toil on the part of many

7

generations. Say not that prejudices are in the way of our making spiritual conquests. What can not enthusiasm and faith accomplish with the aid of God? A few Jewish apostles, poor, unknown, despised, overmastered the proud and mighty Greek and Roman World. We have long enough been hiding our light under a bushel. We have, like Jonah, been fleeing from the presence of God and refused to bring God's message to the children of the world. Let us, even with our feeble power, begin to prepare the day of God. At best it will take centuries and centuries to accomplish the task. But ours is the duty to begin the work and do it with all our heart, all our soul, and all our might. With the all-wise and omnipotent God is left the completion and direction thereof. Let everyone of us consider themselves an apostle of Israel's message to the Gentiles. Let everyone endeavor to demonstrate by their deeds and words the beauty and nobility of character shaped by the forces of Yahvism. Let the conduct of each of us be such that people who are not of the seed of Abraham will be led to worship the one only God and flock to God's sanctuary, that they may learn God's ways and walk in God's paths. It is our duty to understand the ways of God and walk as standard-bearers in the path of Yahvism. Inviting the Gentiles to the house of Yahweh, we must be prepared to tell them, what kind of religion we offer them as the light and guidance of life individual and social. Driven by a sense of supreme duty we undertake, with many misgivings, the difficult task of answering the question: What kind of religion do we offer to the Gentiles?

Hear, O Israel, Yahweh our God, Yahweh is One; thou shalt love thy neighbor as thyself. These two commandments are the vital and central principles of

Yahvism. They are the creative ideas of our religion, from which all other beliefs and moral laws spring. Both together form the supreme idea of Yahvistic faith and ethics. One is the complement of the other. They belong together like heart and head. Without the belief in the absolute unity, perfection, and omnipotence of a supreme Creator, the unity of humanity and universal love have no eternal basis to rest on. Without the idea of the unity of the human race centered in God, and the duty of love flowing from the spiritual kinship of all people, the unity of God is but a useless metaphysical idea. The solidarity and commonwealth of all the families of the earth, in other words, the love of our fellows, is the perfect fruit of Israel's ethical monotheism. The belief in more than one God, the belief in a divine duality or a divine triad or trinity, or the belief in no God or atheism, leads to immorality. Any religion but that which teaches the absolute oneness of the Divine power, is likely to generate feelings, thoughts, and acts of inhumanity.

According to the pagan theory of nature and humanity the universe came into existence and assumed its present form by dint of its own inherent blind energy. The gods themselves were the offspring of nature, subject for good and evil to an inexorable fate, or to an unconscious omnipotent law having its ground outside and above the gods. The world was not the creation of a wise and almighty will. Nature was not the embodiment of a Divine plan of beneficence. The universe was not sanctified and spiritualized by being regarded as the visible revelation of the beauty and love of a holy and all-good spirit. There was no eternal purpose weaving together all forms of existence, all events and times into the living garment of the Deity. Good and evil lay opposite each other in nature, both unexplained and irreconcilable, both accidents, irrational, both acting blindfoldly, capriciously, without a will and without a reason. The gods were merely lucky aristocrats whom a whim of nature had produced and endowed with certain limited powers. They created nothing; their being shed no light on the mystery of existence, nor on the problem of good and evil in nature. They were no types of ideal goodness. On the contrary, they concentrated within themselves all the seeming contradictions of nature, all the wild impulses and cruel freaks, all the apparent brutal selfishness and heartless indifference to suffering. The gods were at war with one another, because each one represented only a part. Each one was the patron, or father and protector, of a limited section of the human race, and stood to the rest of humanity in a relation of hostility. As there was no unity of the Divine power, so there was no unity of humanity. There were as many kinds of people as there were gods, there were as many gods as there were peoples or tribes. Every people looked upon all the others as standing outside the fellowship of its own humanity, because there was to their mind no Divine unity embracing all the children of humanity and welding them together into a family covenant, worshiping the same common Maker and Parent. With profound insight in the origin, nature, and results of idolatry or polytheism, the prophets of Yahweh recognized in it the root of all evil and sin, and hated it as the deadly enemy of humanity, as the natural foe of justice and mercy and holiness. Pagans were habitually unjust, and cruel to all people but members of their own tribe. The reason is obvious enough. The pagan did not regard them as fellow tribesmen. The pagan despised them as inferior beings, sprung from a contemptible ancestry. They did not worship the same gods, nor stand under their protecting egis. The idea of humanity was unknown to pagan civilization. The word "humanitas" meant politeness, urbanity, courteous behavior. Humanity in the broad sense of the spiritual unity of all people has its vital roots in the belief that all races of people have their common origin in one universal God who has dowered them all with equal and unalienable rights, and knit them together in bonds of mutual obligations and loving kindness. Pagans recognized only their compatriots, fellow-citizens, as their true fellows. A person as a person had no worth, no rights, no claims, no duties. The pagan could not, as the Israelite, look with awe upon all people as wonderfully and fearfully made, as beings clothed with the godlike dignity of humanity bestowed upon them by the Spirit of all. Right and duty were merely social laws, legal ordinances. But they had nothing absolute and universal in them, simply because in the pagan theory of the world there was no absolute good will, no universal reason, from which to derive the moral laws as eternal revelations of the Divine attributes. Love was merely physical love, the natural family affections or the sentiment of friendship of one individual for another. But it was not the pure spiritual love of person as person, after the type of the love of God for all mortals; it was not mercy for the finite image of the Eternal whose mercy extends over all Its creatures.

In polytheism sin in its deepest moral and religious sense was unknown. Sin was dreaded because of its evil consequences. It was viewed as an external injurious act and was punished by the human and divine guardians of the state as rebellion against the established ordinances of society. Sin was not an inward self-debasement, a falling away from the infinite moral dignity of humanity dwelling in us, a willful breaking away from the life of God, in which we are to share by walking with God in God's ways. Sin was simply an infraction of a statute. It would cease to be sin if the powers that be, divine and human, chose to reverse the statute. Sin is not, according to pagan theology, absolutely abominable, because it is a departure from the holiness and perfection of the one only God, the life and essence of all being. It is not rebellion against the everlasting canons of universal love.

Polytheism must foster vice; for it springs from the belief that the different parts of nature have separate lives and powers and are represented by various gods who have the qualities of the phenomena they stand for and typify. Every part of nature that is worshiped must be obeyed. The bestial impulses, as well as the cruelties and tortures inflicted by nature, are manifestations of divine powers, which should be imitated by people. Hence, the monstrous practices of idolatrous nations against which the writers of the Old Testament and of the New hurl their fierce denunciations.

As has been said before, the pagan mind could make no serious attempt to solve the problem of good and evil. For in polytheism neither good nor evil had a reason for existence, because they could not be conceived as rooted in universal existence. No one God, nor all the gods together, had created the world. Hence no god could be believed to be the source of all good nor of all evil in nature and history. There was no almighty being, in whose manifestations good and evil were pitted as contrasts. Good and evil fell apart as causeless, purposeless, and meaningless phenomena. There was no room in polytheism for the hope that evil would in the fullness of time be overcome and rooted out of the world, since there was no omnipotent power of good to accomplish it. To the pagan mind the history of nature and of humanity was merely a succession of events. It did not begin in all-wise and all-good omnipotent Will, nor would it end in the unfolding and victory of the universal good. We must not, however, fail to recognize in polytheism the germs of true religion, the beginnings of an exalted ethics of humanity.

Germs of Religious and Ethical Truth in Polytheism

Taking a broad view of the spiritual history of humanity as one continuous life and growth, we can not but believe that polytheism, too, was a revelation of the Infinite, a necessary stage in the unfolding of the spirit of God in the human race. God has left no children without a ray of God's light. The ways of God through all the domain of nature and of mind are those of gradual evolution from lower to ever higher forms, from the imperfect to the more perfect, from faint streaks of dawning truth unto the brightness of the perfect day. But of this we shall speak more fully when we come to treat of the subject of Revelation and religious development. In believing that a divine being was indwelling, and presiding over, every part and phenomenon of nature, polytheism gave expression to the truth that Nature is no weltering mass of blind matter, no soulless mechanism, but is quick with conscious life and full of superhuman divine power. This is an immense gain made for true religion. In fact, monotheism could not have arisen at all, if the pagan theory of the world had not prepared the fruitful parent idea, out of which grew the belief in one almighty all-pervading Intelligence, the Maker, Preserver, and Ruler of heaven and earth and all they contain.

The human mind, even in its undeveloped religious stage, in the polytheistic state, had grasped the fundamental idea on which all religion and philosophy will forever rest; the idea namely: mind, life, feeling, will power, thought is not confined to the brain of people and animals; it is not absolutely bound up with a bodily frame. Conscious life exists outside of people and animals and manifests its energy in every possible form, visible or invisible, of the external world. Again, the conscious life did not for the first time in the existence of the world make its appearance in people and their inferior fellowcreatures. Gods, similar in character, qualities, loves, and hates to person or beast but superior to them in power and length of days, have existed in the heavens above and the earth beneath and in the waters under the earth, long before the human race or any animate being had been born on this globe. The monotheism of the prophets in its highest reaches, still firmly roots in this primary spiritual belief, in the belief of the pagans. For the central idea of our faith is: A universal creative Intelligence animates and pervades all nature; before the mountains were brought forth and the earth was born, and the world, even from Eternity to Eternity God was God.

The fact is, the belief that there are in the external world entities, powers, activities, and tendencies like those which distinguish the inner world of mind, lies at the very root of all religious knowledge, is the necessary condition of all truth. Without this pre-supposition, truth cognition would be impossible. How could the mind comprehend the world without, if that world had nothing in common with mind? How could the intelligence have any knowledge of nature, if nature were not somehow assumed to be related to intelligence? How could the things of nature be translated into thought, if they were not believed to be written in the characters of thought and could not be spelled out by the mind?

The most primitive people unconsciously started in all their thoughts, beliefs, and fantastic vagaries from this cardinal truth. The most advanced minds of prophets and philosophers base all knowledge and all faith upon this root-principle of the intelligence. The worshipers of Baal and Astarte and other gods shared the belief in mind-like powers existing and acting in nature outside of man, with the prophets of Yahweh, who is the spirit of all spirits, the cause and ground of all being. With this far-reaching difference however: in polytheism consciousness, intelligence, will, in nature is broken up into a vast number of separate beings, into a teeming multitude of divine personalities or gods. Every part of nature exists by itself and for itself, and in and above every part there is a divine being, the conscious counterpart of the material object. In the monotheism of the prophets all nature is one in origin, cause, and purpose, a living rational unity, a growing harmony in Yahweh, the universal Reason, the creative almighty Will, in whom all things and all spirits live, move, and have their being.

It is, of course, impossible to explain the rise of moral monotheism in Israel by showing its points of connection with polytheism. Just as little can Humanity be explained by pointing out the links of kinship subsisting between people and apes. But it is in every respect important to know the basis of truth common to the partially developed and to the most highly evolved religion, and to bring into view the manifold service rendered by polytheism in preparing the seed and the soil for monotheism.

In its own crude and materialistic way polytheism taught with the utmost emphasis the fundamental religious truth that people stand in closest relations to their God and that a person's nature is of kin to that of the Deity. Practically this belief is the most important, the most influential of all religious doctrines. It brings down religion from the region of mere speculation and makes it the most human of all affairs. It elevates a person to the Divine and brings the Divine down to the heart and into the very home of each person. This faith has built an ideal ladder between heaven and earth on which divine powers descend to mortal people, to protect, instruct them, and impart dignity to their lives, and on which again mortals ascend to share in the qualities, in the aims, and the glory of the Divinity. Each person is godlike, each person is a child of the Deity—this was the intuitive faith alike of paganism and Yahvism. Only, the pagans took their godlikeness and their descent from the divine in a literal and physical sense. The members of every family, of every tribe and people believed themselves, in the material acceptation of the word, to be lineal descendants of their ancestral god, to have the blood of their divine forebear and ruler in their veins. As their gods were identical with visible parts of nature, so was, in their opinion, the relationship between people and their deity of a naturalistic and sensuous kind. The bond of union between them mainly the kinship of animalism. Still, low as was the pagan conception of the mutual relations between a people and their god, it was yet the fruitful germ out of which there arose in the religion of the prophets the sublime conception of people being made after the spiritual likeness and in the moral similitude of the Sovereign God of all spirits, of Yahweh, the creative Reason and Love. Countless ages had believed that a people was the physical image and offspring of its gods. Thereby the human mind was prepared to receive the message of monotheism that each person is the spiritual image of the perfect Spirit, that the soul of each person is a lamp of God, that Divine love and human righteousness are the true ties of kinship between the Creator and the creature. Thus polytheism is also in this respect seen to have been the natural precursor and path-maker of monotheism. There is no break in the development of the spirit of humanity. Even the greatest spiritual revolution, the victorious rise of monotheism in Israel, was an evolution from pre-existing forms of belief, and an involution of what was truest and best in the religious life of former ages.

This is evident from other points of organic contact and transition between polytheism and monotheism. Take the case of idol-worship or the adoration of images representing gods in human form. The vast majority of the human race has from time immemorial to this day been clinging to idolatry, a mode of worship which the prophets denounced as the abomination of abominations, and which we too can not help regarding as a blasphemous and degrading practice. But we must be broad enough to recognize that idolatry helped on the religious education of the race. By presenting the gods to the eye of the worshiper in the figure of people, though of superhuman stature and majesty, it impressed upon the mind of the believer that the dread ruling powers of nature were related in their being and ways to people and that they possessed the attributes of humanity. For thousands and thousands of years the worship of the Divine under the symbol of a person, the highest and noblest of all known creatures, tended in the eyes of the worshipers to humanize and moralize the gods and to vary them, in appearance and action, from the beast-gods and the bird-gods of still older and lower religions. The ground was thus prepared by idolatry for the sublime conception and the pure worship of God as taught by the prophets of Yahweh. God is not a person or the son of a person. God is unlike anything visible or material. Nothing corporeal and mortal should be compared to God, though it can be exalted in beauty above all created things. But the spirit of each person is the symbol of the Eternal, the soul of each person is the faint image of the universal Soul, the moral qualities of each person are a revelation of the attributes of God's perfection. In other words, God is most like that which is highest, holiest, and most divine in each person; like reason shining in darkness, like justice crushing the head of oppression, like love going forth to all flesh. Having gained an absolute victory within the Jewish church, monotheism may now without fear of danger freely acknowledge the debt of gratitude which it owes to the preparatory work and influence of idolatry.

The belief in an all-wise and all-just Divine Providence shaping the destinies of individuals and nations, quickening humanity to ever higher ends, may be traced to its humble and child-like beginnings in primitive religion, and be followed along its upward course through the great religions of Asia and of classic antiquity. The pagans of all times and climes had their tutelary god always with them, dwelling with them under their roof as the divine sovereign and parent of the household. The family god watched over its human children, shielded them from evil, warned them against danger, and looked out for their good. This was certainly special providence in the most literal sense. Every tribe, every people, believed itself to be under the perpetual jurisdiction and guidance of its tribal or national god. Every people carried on the business of life in peace and war in the firm conviction that the eye of their god was observing them, that the god's wisdom was leading them, and the god's power rendering them help. Monotheism took over this inspiring belief as an heritage from the religious past of humanity. What a wonderful transformation this belief underwent in the monotheistic atmosphere of Yahvism, the religion of humanity! The providence the pagans believed in was selfish, narrow, tribal, unjust, and shortsighted. Providence was favoritism. The tutelary god had a personal interest in protecting its people or its worshiper. Vast numbers of people in our day are in this respect, as in so many other regards, thorough pagans. The rulers, priests, and writers of every people speak of God as if God were the special Protector and Providence of their favorite nation and cared very little for the rest of humanity. They sing solemn Te Deums for victories vouchsafed them by *their* God; they intone hymns of thanksgiving to *their* God who fought their battles and helped them to slaughter thousands and tens of thousands of human beings. The Providence of the prophets is no respecter of persons or of nations. Yahweh guides by Yahweh's counsel all individuals, and all the tribes of humanity. All people are alike God's children and God's care and mercy extend over all God's creatures. In polytheism there are many providences which are at war with one another. There are as many providences as there are families and peoples. In the religion of Israel's monotheism there is one God, one humanity, one impartial and all-loving Providence, universal, unfailing, all-wise. Still, if the families of the earth had not for countless generations been accustomed to trust in a tribal and egotistical providence, the prophets of Yahweh probably would not have been able to imbue people with the belief that the eye of one only God is upon all God's children, that all humanity is being led by God toward ideal goals.

The Unity of Humanity

The idea of an inalienable and indestructible right inherent in every individual, the idea of a divine right to life, liberty, property, and the pursuit of happiness vested in every person by virtue of their godlike personality, the idea of justice wide as humanity, holy and awful as God, is the cardinal ethical principle of Yahvism. To secure the equal rights of all people because all are equal before their common Maker, to enforce the inviolable dignity and sanctity of every human being because each is the spiritual image of the Most High, to inculcate the infinite importance of meting out justice in private and social life, to rich and poor, to the native and the stranger, with an impartial hand, this is the chiefest burden of the Prophets, this is the deathless mission of the religion which we offer to the Gentiles. This principle of universal justice without regard to kinship, nationality, and creed, the love of right and equity passing the love of life itself, the hatred of injustice and oppression stronger than death, spring from the two cardinal beliefs of prophetic monotheism, from the belief in the absolute oneness and goodness of God and the belief in the unity of humanity centered in an all-just Creator, Lawgiver, and Judge. These beliefs are the ultimate source of right, the living fountain from which justice flows for all the children of the world. According to every other theology, with the sole exception of the religion of Yahweh, humanity is broken up into several parts, which are separated by distinctions of race or nationality, or marked off from one another by religious differences. According to every other theory of the world and of society, the fullness of human rights is conditioned upon the accident of birth, upon community of descent or community of faith or upon both. To the Athenian only a full-blooded Greek who worshiped the gods of Hellas was a genuine person and alone was entitled to the fullness of human rights. The outside barbarians were not in the opinion of the Athenian full people. They possessed no rights which the high-caste Greeks, the favorites of the Olympian gods, were in conscience bound to respect. They held their life and property only on sufferance. Whatever rights of protection they enjoyed, while dwelling among the Greeks, were accorded to them as an act of grace by the Hellenic gods and their privileged worshipers. Closely examined, among those believing in more than one god right is merely a privilege, a prerogative granted by some Divine Power to those the god loves. For how can a god who is not the Sovereign and Parent of all people command laws of justice that shall be binding on all people? How can a being, who is not itself absolute and eternal, be the author of absolute statutes of righteousness and of everlasting ordinances of right? How can social right and equity be derived from a god who is itself believed to be constantly at war with other gods and with people? The moral laws and the ideals of the perfect life can not derive their sanction from gods who are themselves held to be imperfect and tainted with selfishness and cruelty.

The idea of universal justice can be cherished, and the attempt to realize it be made, only by people who firmly believe in one universal God, in an absolute righteous Will, an infinite Power that is perfect in all Its ways. Justice in the true sense of broadest humanity was unknown and inconceivable outside Israel. It was unknown even in Israel before it was conceived in all its depth and grandeur by the prophets and proclaimed by them and defended in the face of fierce opposition offered by the rich and powerful. Justice was, therefore, everywhere except in the ideal world of prophetic monotheism, merely an extension of the mutual relation subsisting between the members of the family group to a wider circle. All the members of the city or state were regarded as relations, and were expected to deal with one another as family. All people who were beyond the pale of the assumed family were outcasts and outlaws. In this respect, as in so many others, the Chinese are the most consistent, the most ancient and pagan of all nations. The whole theory and practice of Chinese social order rests on the family idea. All Chinese are officially and religiously considered as kin, as members of one huge family. The emperor is obeyed and venerated as the parent, priest, and lawgiver of all subjects. The emperor is, in official parlance and in the language and belief of the masses, held to be a lineal descendant of the heaven-god and the earth-goddess.

According to the teachings of unadulterated Christianity, according to the dogmatic theology of the Trinitarian churches, there is really no unity of mankind, neither with God in heaven nor with people on earth, neither in this world nor in the world beyond the grave. Those who believe in God the Parent, God the Christ, and the Holy Ghost, those who believe in the redeeming death and saving blood of the Savior, are family in Christ Jesus; they alone are saved and exalted; they alone are called the children of God. They enjoy the favor of the God the Parent and are the beloved of the Christ. They are visited, purified, and sanctified by the Holy Ghost. For them are reserved the bountiful blessings of Divine grace and love. They are saved from the power of evil in this world and they are sure to enter Paradise in the hereafter. But those who refuse to believe in the Trinity and in the sacrificial death of Jesus, because their reason and faith can not accept such a dogma, stand outside the consecrated precincts of the Christian commonwealth. They are strangers to God and strangers to the community of Jesus Christ. They are separated by a vast gulf from the congregation of God. They are not at one with their Maker, because they lack the mediation of Christ's atoning love. They live unredeemed and unblessed on earth, and in the hereafter they will through all eternity suffer untold torments as a deserved punishment for having lacked the true faith and for having wantonly declined the proffered means of salvation. On one side stand the wretched non-Christian goats, and on the other the blessed Christian lambs. Would you call this a real unity of humanity in one all-just and all-loving God?

Christian philosophers are asserting with endless reiteration and infinite unction, that of all religions Christianity alone proclaimed the unity of humanity and the commonwealth of all people. But the Christianity which they thus glorify is not really Christianity. They sail under false colors. They make a false use of the name Christianity which they first emptied of all its true and distinctive contents. Smitten with judicial blindness as to the religion of Israel, swayed by narrow inherited prejudices, they first misrepresent Yahvism in a spirit of willful ignorance and rob it of its glory and merit. They take the imperishable religious truth, the doctrine of the unity and godlike dignity of all people, and give it the name of Christianity and pit it against the faith of Israel as something infinitely higher and diviner. They are self-deceiving deceivers. Sure it is, Jesus was a teacher of Yahvism and not of Christianity. Sure it is, Jesus was no Christian in the Trinitarian sense, and in any other sense there is no Christian religion. Jesus taught the unity of humanity just like the other prophets and wise men of Israel. But Trinitarian Christianity rejects the unity and commonwealth of humanity in the sense it was revealed by God through God's prophets. Humanity is divided into two distinct parts, into those who believe in the blessed Trinity and those who deny it, or have never heard of it. The latter are abandoned of God, no fountain of grace for them, no treasures of salvation in store for them. The Holy Spirit is not in them, though they walk in the ways of righteousness and long to be perfect with their God. The curse of original sin rests upon them and keeps their soul in a state of degradation. They have not been recognized by God the Parent by acquiring, through faith, a share in the great sacrifice of atonement made by Jesus. They are not born again to the life spiritual in Christ through the miracle of baptism. They are the unregenerate children of Adam and form a lower, purely carnal species of humanity. High above this division of fallen and unbelieving humanity are the children of light and faith, the

24

blessed of God, the living members of the body of
Christ.   Again and again they renew their life by
assimilating to themselves through the mystery of the
communion the flesh and the blood of the Redeemer.
They alone are the true people of God. To them has
been vouchsafed dominion and glory and wisdom. To
them the earth has been given as an inheritance. They
are the true heirs to whatever things beautiful, to
whatever things true, and whatever things good have
been accomplished in ages past by all nations and
religions, by the prophets, poets, thinkers, and truth-
seeking heroes of all times.   All peoples, all
civilizations have toiled and plowed and sown that the
Christian commonwealth may reap a rich harvest. The
rest of humanity, unredeemed, unregenerate, inferior,
are weltering in religious darkness and pining away in
spiritual poverty outside the Christian city of God.
They exist on sufferance, and the followers of Christ
are their superiors and rulers by the grace of God. The
pagans, the Jews, and so-called infidels are children of
the handmaidens, but the Christians are children of
the true spouse, the church of Christ Jesus.

Such is the unity of humanity which genuine
Christianity, which the Trinitarian churches teach. It
is infinitely superior to the pagan conception of
humanity. In paganism the distinction between one
person and another, one tribe and another, is of a
physical and racial nature. There is, theoretically at
least, no possibility of members of one people or race
crossing the lines of separation and blending with
those of another. In Christianity the distinction is
spiritual, religious. Any person, whatever their people
and race, may become a Christian and share in the
privileges of grace and prerogatives of salvation of the
chosen part of humanity. No bars are raised against

any person, whatever their descent; no wall shuts any person from the Christian community. The gates are wide to all comers. Still the distinction between one person and another is there deep and far-reaching. The separation between one part of humanity and the other is due to Divine favoritism, not to Divine justice. It is by an arbitrary act of God that vast numbers of people are doomed to moral degradation and spiritual death, because their reason can not accept the dogma of the Trinity and the other central Christian doctrines. On the other hand, God exalts those who choose to believe in the Christian mysteries, and brings them nigh unto God and pours out upon them all God's mercy and crowns them with loving kindness. This is indeed election with divine vengeance. The Calvinistic dogma of election is the most logical and consistent expression of the more general Christian belief in Divine election or favoritism. In Calvinism there are but a few lucky mortals whom the whim of the Deity picks out for salvation and blessedness, while the rest are left to perish in spite of their correct belief. In the Catholic Church all Roman Catholics are chosen and saved. Even the broadest Trinitarian churches teach that a yawning gulf separates the worshipers of Christ from those who deny Him.

The Christian theory which separates one person from another according to creed, which divides humanity into two distinct parts, into God-abandoned deniers of the divinity of Jesus and into the redeemed children of the triune God, has done as much mischief as the pagan principle of kinship and tribal divinities. As long as the Trinitarian dogma of salvation and election was firmly believed in, it sowed everywhere the baneful seeds of disunion and hatred and was the parent of infinite woes, physical and mental. The spiritual pride and selfishness of people caused the practice to come up to and surpass the theory. From the time Trinitarian Christianity ascended the throne and became mistress of the Western world until the spirit of Yahvistic humanity began to resist and restrain it, the pagans, the heretics, the Jews, and the Muslims were held not to be equal to the Christians before God and the law, and were treated accordingly with pitiless injustice and often with remorseless cruelty. True, even in the darkest days of the Middle Ages Christianity did a vast deal toward elevating and humanizing the masses. The Church tried to knit together many nations and races and kingdoms into a spiritual commonwealth. But those outside the Christian church were dealt with in a spirit of contempt and harsh exclusiveness. Attributing to the God-head the injustice of loving and saving the orthodox believer, and abhorring and condemning the unbelievers, the Christians strove to walk in the ways of the Almighty. For this reason they had diverse measures of justice for Christians and non-Christians, or rather the Christian alone was believed to have an indefeasible claim to human rights and the privileges of the human commonwealth. Even in our day the spirit of universal justice, the spirit of all-embracing humanity, such as lived and worked miracles of salvation through the prophets from Moses down to Jesus, is far from having completely triumphed over the medieval spirit of superstitious pride and intolerance. The Christian still believes that a Christian stands nearer to the throne and heart of God and possesses larger rights than Jews, Muslims, and pagans. And what a Christian believes is still practiced to a large extent. At best the non-Christian is contemptuously accorded tolerance. Where the non-Christian enjoys equal rights, it is considered a gracious concession made by the ruling Christian. But the non-Christian is not regarded as the peer of the Christians, in moral dignity and social worth.

Woe betide the non-Christians, the pagans or the Muslim, if wrong is done by one of them to Christians in any part of the world! If a few hundred rebellious Christian subjects of the Turk are killed by their wrathful rulers, all Christendom burns with righteous indignation and demands immediate and fullest redress. The remonstrances made by the Christian powers are backed up by a million Christian guns. But when five million Jews in Russia are deprived of all human rights, treated as pariahs, plundered, tormented beyond endurance, driven from their homes and made to perish body and soul, the Christian powers raise no protest against these horrors enacted by a Christian potentate against helpless human beings, "They are only Jews," the Christian says in his heart, "they are not our family."

Lately a few Christian missionaries were killed in China by an infuriated mob. A cry of horror was heard through the length and breadth of Christendom. Vengeance for the Christian blood ruthlessly shed was demanded in Europe and America. The warships of the great Christian nations hurried to the scene of slaughter. Powerful arguments—a thousand cannons—were used with the helpless emperor. And they had their effect. A large number of Chinese have been beheaded in expiation of the crime against the missionaries. This was justice, sure enough, claimed and obtained by Christians for Christians. But scores of Chinese have at sundry times been massacred in America, hundreds have again and again been plundered and driven from their homes by Christian mobs. Still there was no national indignation in America against these monstrous acts. No European people remonstrated with our government against these brutal outrages. A paltry sum was paid by our government to the relations of the helpless victims. They were only heathen Chinese. Their lives and rights do not weigh much in the scales of justice. An editorial writer in one of our great newspapers recently said, "One Anglo-Saxon Christian is worth as much as six heathen Chinese. Six lives should be given for one Christian life." Verily, this is a beautiful illustration of the unity of humanity, a noble realization of universal justice. The moral disease of anti-Semitism which is raging on the continent of Europe and disgracing modern civilization is due to two co-operating causes, one pagan, the other Christian, in origin and scope. The fanatics of race and nationality, the Aryomaniacs, say: " Jew ought to be stripped of all civil and political rights, and if possible, be driven from the land, because they are not of our blood and race." This argument has a pagan pedigree. "The Jew should in every way be restricted and restrained and systematically excluded in public and private life from fellowship with Christians. The Jews are a thorn in the thigh of our Christian civilization because they differ from us in faith, and observe an attitude of open or concealed hostility toward our Savior." Thus reason the fanatics who consider themselves appointed by God to watch over the highest interests of Christianity. Opposite the polytheistic as well as the Trinitarian conceptions of humanity which separate one person from another according to physical kinship or according to religious differences, stands Yahvism with its unshakable belief in the indestructible unity, both physical and spiritual, of all the families of the earth. Opposite the theory and practice of justice both of paganism and of Christianity, which base all right either on community of blood or community of faith, stands the religion of ethical monotheism with its eternal principle of universal, indiscriminating justice, with its solemn declaration that all people are equal, because all are made in the spiritual image of God. Yahvism recognizes no distinctions of race or differences of religious belief before the throne of Divine and human justice. All human beings are declared to be alike the children of the household of God. In the city of God, as seen by the eye of the prophets, there are no favorites endowed with rights superior to those of the humblest child of humanity. This would be a grievous injustice done by God. The spirit of the prophets, their deathless love of righteousness, will brook no injustice, no partiality in God. The throne of Yahweh must be established on justice, or the true Israelite would refuse to prostrate themselves at God's feet. The true Israelite would not adore a God in whom there is unrighteousness, but would turn away with indignation and despair from the supreme Power, were the Power conclusively proved to bestow God's favors with an unjust hand, to deal with people according to caprice, and not to reward and love every person according to the righteousness of their ways.

This idea is the very soul of our religion. Justice is absolute, eternal, and universal, and is binding on God and on people and all rational beings, wherever and under whatever conditions they may exist in any part of the universe. God is justice; this is God's name forever. If God were not just God would not be God. God would be a dread power, feared by weak mortals, but God would not deserve our worship and love. The sacred writers never weary of praising and invoking the justice of God. The righteousness of Yahweh is the dearest theme of the Psalmist's song and the chief burden of the Prophet's message. "Thou lovest justice," say the sweet singers of Israel, "Thy right hand is full of justice." Justice walks before God. Justice and judgment are the foundations of God's throne. God's justice is everlasting, all God's ordinances are just. Yahweh is righteous in all ways. Yahweh judges the whole world in justice. In the song of Moses it is said: Just and upright is God. In his confessions of Israel's sins, Ezra says: O Yahweh, God of Israel, Thou art just. Nehemiah prays: Thou hast kept thy promise, because Thou art righteous. Thou art just in all that is brought upon us; for Thou hast done right, but we have done wickedly.

But why multiply instances? The belief in the perfect justice of God permeates every part of the Bible. It has molded the ethics of Yahvism and determined the course of Israel's history. So convinced were the leaders of religious thought in Israel, that the Maker of heaven and earth must be righteous in all ways and just toward all people, that the heroes of faith do not hesitate to turn to Yahweh and demand justice at Yahweh's hand, whenever Yahweh seems to be doing injustice to them or to other people. "Shall the judge of the whole world not do justice?" said Abraham, the friend of God, the parent of the faithful, while pleading with God for the people of Sodom and Gomorrah. If there are only fifty or forty or even ten righteous people in the doomed cities, God should spare all for the sake of the righteous that are in their midst. For it would be wrong to let the righteous perish with the wicked. It would be unjust not to give the good time to change by their example the life of the sinful and reclaim them from the evil of their way.

Jeremiah, the martyr prophet, being ruthlessly persecuted by his cruel enemies and treacherously treated by his brethren, challenges God in the bitterness of his heart and dares enter into a controversy with Him:

Thou art righteous, O Yahweh, when I contend with Thee.

Why does the way of the wicked prosper?

Why are all the people of treachery at ease?

Thou has planted them, yea, they have taken root.

They grow, yea, they bring forth fruit,

Thou art near to their mouth, but far from their hearts.

But Thou, O Yahweh, knowest me;

Thou hast seen me and tried my heart.

Whether it be devoted to Thee.

In the agony of his sufferings Job calls God to account for afflicting him without just cause. I would speak to the Almighty! he cries, I desire to reason with God. "Behold, God may slay me, but I will defend my ways before God. Behold, I have arranged my plea, I know that I shall prove my right."

This heroic love of justice, this dauntless conviction that wrong is wrong whether done by a person or by God, the sublime belief that the ways of God must be just and righteous altogether, form the keynote to the theology and the ethics of the religion of Israel. From the first day of its appearance among the children of the world Yahvism has above all things been the religion of righteousness, the religion of justice uncompromising and universal, of justice

Divine and human. The fruitful germ of Yahvism was deadly hatred of wrong done to the weak by the strong, by the rich to the poor, by the native to the stranger, a horror of aristocratic privileges and abuses, a fierce anger against oppression practiced in the name of gods, of caste, of race and nationality. The tree of Yahvism had from the very beginning its roots in infinite pity for the downtrodden, in profound reverence for the humanity of all people, in a quenchless love of justice as broad as humanity. Yahvism, the religion of humanity, is a perennial battle for the right. So it was conceived by Moses, so it was revealed by him to his immediate followers, and so it was transmitted by him and the other prophets to be a heritage to all generations.

This essay was originally published in slightly different form in January 1896.

CHAPTER 2

The Reasons Why I Believe In God

LET us begin our search after the rational grounds of our belief in God. Let us seek for proofs, if haply they may be found, that there exists an all-pervading, eternal Unity Divine which embraces both the universe and the soul. Let us try to bring into clear view cogent reasons for believing in a Supreme Being, in an ultimate Reality and Creative Energy of which matter and mind, force and will, the external world of nature and the inner world of consciousness, are perennial manifestations and purposeful self-revelations. Let us for the moment discard all preconceived beliefs and unbeliefs and in all seriousness and solemnity face the problem of problems, as if we were commissioned by humanity to find a solution to it; as if our age depended on us to give a satisfactory answer to the question, compared with which all other questions dwindle into utter insignificance.

We know two kinds of existence, the external material world of things, of objects, and the internal world of consciousness, of feelings, thoughts, and ideas. The most awful mystery of all is this very mystery of existence itself. How comes there to be anything at all, matter and motion, atoms, forces, life inanimate and animate? How comes there to be feeling, sensation, thought, or consciousness? Space and infinitude, the home of all being, time and eternity, the stream in which all that exists and happens moves, rises to the surface and disappears; what are they, why are they, why can not we imagine them as nonexistent? To be, the eternal, indestructible fact of being in general, of existence universal, beginningless, endless, continuous, that is the question.

We can by no effort of ours bring ourselves to deny that something exists somehow, somewhere. Even if we think that all things outside ourselves are unreal appearances, that this fair world, the heavens and the earth are merely a dream of our mind, yet we doubters and dreamers still exist. You can not think of a time when there was absolutely nothing in existence, nor are you able to think of a time when existence itself shall be annihilated. Take the wings of imagination and fly from star-system to star-system to the uttermost bounds of all known galaxies, beyond the region of the faintest and remotest cosmic cloud, even in the heart of eternal night and silence and cold you are still floating on the waves of being, and are unable to break away from your soul's inseparable companion, from the idea of omnipresent existence. Should you fancy space beyond all stellar regions to be absolutely empty, still space is left, space exists. You can put no bound to space in thought. Beyond the uttermost reach of imagination infinitude stretches, one, indivisible, eternal, pregnant with the seeds of star-births, heaving with the throbs of universal force. You can not conceive a limit set to force. You can not say, only to a certain point in space does it go and can not dart beyond a certain fixed boundary line. Where force is, there dwells being, there are beating the pulses of all-pervading energy. Being, then, has no limits in space or time. Existence is infinite and eternal. Well may the idea of infinite and eternal existence thrill us with religious awe, and cause us to observe towards it an attitude of speechless wonder. It is the simplest and surest and most universal fact. It is the taproot of all truths. It underlies all thoughts.

Without the idea of existence nothing is imaginable, thinkable, nothing is possible. Yet it is the mystery of mysteries. We are so near it, it surrounds us, we live, move, and have our being in it. Still it is inscrutable. We are overwhelmed by the thought that whatever is has always been and forever will be. We prostrate ourselves before the unfathomable mystery that matter and force, the very atoms and energies with which we are everywhere in closest touch, of which we ourselves form a living part, have existed through boundless space from eternity to eternity. Before the race of humanity was born, before the sun, the moon, and the stars were formed, there was the same essence, the same indwelling power was moving through space, combining, dissolving, blossoming, bearing fruit, decaying and awakening to new life and activity through seeming death.

The same substance, the same force, the same laws existed on and on, indestructible, of the self-same identity, ere the universe blossomed into its present living harmony as at this very hour.

Some of the profoundest religious minds of former days have stood like us in worshiping awe before the unfathomable mystery of beginningless, endless, and universal being. They, too, wrestled with the attempt to comprehend the incomprehensible, to express the inexpressible. They adored the infinite and eternal being as the highest Being, as the only Reality. They worshiped it as the supreme Power behind all power, as the permanent essence behind all fleeting appearances. The Bible calls the Supreme Being Yahweh, "He who is, was, and forever will be." The Most High was revealed to Moses as "I Am that I Am," "I Am, that is my name." In the theosophical speculations of the later Vedic poets the all-pervading, self-existent essence is worshiped under the name of Brahma. Some of the greatest Greek philosophers called God the Being, *to on,* or the true Being, *to ontos on.*

* * * * *

We have so far considered the mystery of existence in itself, in a purely abstract way. We have been dealing only with the bare, though awe-inspiring, fact that something infinite and eternal does exist, that something, be it matter, force, mind, has always been, still is, and forever will be. But the question of questions is: Is all existence of one essence, are all forms of being one being, all forces one force, all manifestations of energy the outpourings of one eternal Energy? Are all minds lights reflected from the effulgence of one infinite Self? Does the chain of natural causes and effects begin and terminate in a highest cause, in an almighty cause of causes? Is there unity and identity of essence in all diversity of being and multiplicity of forms?

May it not be that every atom has from all eternity been an isolated self-existent being, an individual independent center of force? Thus there would be an infinity of eternal, uncaused existences. We would then have no principle of all-pervading, all-embracing unity which we are seeking and which is to be accounted the first cardinal attribute of the one only Being, of the ultimate Reality.

Nature, as known even to the most superficial observers, shows the assumption of an infinite number of unrelated atoms without any communication with one another to be the wildest of errors, the most senseless of all imaginable blunders. The universe does not present itself to the human mind as a host of countless self-imprisoned, unresponsive atoms and forces which have no relation to one another, which exert no influence upon one another, and do not mutually determine one another. If every atom were absolutely shut up within itself, if all were not bound up by an indwelling principle of unity, they would not be able to combine with and interpenetrate one another. There would be no change whatever. For all change is caused by the chemical marriage of atoms with atoms, of molecules with molecules, and by the thousand other influences which all elements exercise upon all others, be they near or far. There would be no room for the universal play of cause and effect, if there were no eternal kinship, no inborn love between all elements and forces. How could all the parts of the universe, the remotest and the nearest, be connected together as an harmonious whole by the interminable chain of cause and effect, if there subsisted no eternal relationship between them?

The law of causality is of universal validity and admits of no exception. The underlying principle of all science, the supreme truth, upon which all the systems of knowledge rest, is the indestructible belief, that nothing happens within the whole compass of existence, that nothing can take place in the life of nature and man, without an efficient cause. Every fact is the offspring of other facts which have gone before it and stand to it in the relation of parent cause, and every new fact must give birth to others which in their turn are bound to be the seeds of events to come. Nothing great or small that exists or occurs in the universe stands apart by itself, has the roots of its origin and activity in itself alone. Whatever is or happens is joined together by a chain of cause and effect with every part and force in nature and with the remotest past of the world's life. The whole present with all its countless phenomena, with all its multitudinous forms, is the child of the past by an endless succession of evolutions, which are bound up together and determined by the indestructible ties of universal causation. All the myriad stars and the fullness thereof form a living harmony, a symphony of forces and movements, of action and interaction, of cosmic growth and fruit-bearing. They ebb and flow together with the all-penetrating currents of omnipresent causation. They are interlaced and intertwined by the unbreakable chains of universal order.

Now the question arises: Why must all kinds of existence obey the law of cause and effect? Why are all atoms, all things, all phenomena, all manifestations of force of every kind, held in the eternal embrace of causality? There must be an all-sufficient reason why all things must act and react upon one another. There must be an efficient reason why all particles of matter or atoms influence one another in a certain unalterable manner, why they combine with one another according to fixed laws which they can not transgress. Why is the behavior of all things toward all others subject to an unchangeable rule and order? On what ultimate ground does the law of causality rest?

It is clear that the law of their mutual behavior, the necessity of acting in a certain way in harmonious co-operation with one another, must lie in the original constitution of all the elements of nature.

Now, if the atoms were from all eternity self-centered individual beings, if they were absolutely the last elements and forms of existence behind which there is no higher reality and controlling power, how should they come to form among themselves those everlasting bonds of friendship, to establish the unchangeable laws of their conduct toward one another? Did all the atoms in the starless foretime once meet in counsel, and did they say to one another: "It will not do for us to remain forever in our state of single existence and unprofitable isolation. We must form an everlasting and perfect union. Let us establish among ourselves a covenant which shall not pass away. Let us unite our forces for ever higher ends. Let us lay down for ourselves inviolable laws to which we shall all yield unquestioning obedience. Let us regulate for all eternity our mutual relations. Let us give up our barren independence and through universal interdependence become fruitful, creative. Let the act of one always affect the others in a certain foreordained way. Let us combine and grow into suns, star-systems, earths, plants, animals, and at last flower into man, who shall translate our elemental compact into thought and call our unchangeable social contract the universal law of causality"?

Surely, the indissoluble unity which binds all atoms together into a living harmony, the immutable laws which hold absolute sway over them all, and determine with unfailing precision all their courses, combinations, dissolutions, evolutions, give proof that the atoms can not be separate and self-determined entities, that they can not be the last elements of existence. There can be but one conclusion: Behind all atoms there is one universal Reality, behind all special forms of existence there is one all-enfolding absolute Existence; behind all finite beings there is one infinite Being. All forces are the manifestations of one almighty Force. This supreme Reality, this infinite Essence and omnipotent Power, we call God. All the world-systems are borne in the same parental arms of this one creative Force. They all rest as children, grown or growing, against the bosom of the same infinite parent Power. All their vital energies and unfolding lives are but incarnations and transformations of the one self-identical Energy, inscrutable, all-sustaining, all-quickening, all-pervading. All atoms and aggregations of atoms must obey the eternal and immutable laws of the universal Self, because they are indwelling parts of it; because they live, move, and have their being in it. All nature proceeds from the same divine Essence; the whole Cosmos has blossomed forth from the same omnipotent Energy. Hence no atom, no finite part, no creature, no star can separate itself from the identity of the Almighty, can break away from the immanent modes and ways of infinite Life. The universal reign of law is nothing but the universal self-revelation of the One infinite and unchangeable Power which is forever at one with itself. The universal law of causality flows from the identity of the one omnipresent and omnipotent Being. The unity of nature springs from, and reflects, the unity of God.

* * * * *

Our argument has so far led us only to the necessary belief in a universal, self-existent Essence, to the idea of an infinite, all-enfolding divine Unity, to the conception of an almighty Power which is the ultimate cause of all that is and happens. The truth which we have brought into light forms the first broad foundation on which all religion rests. And now there arises the most far-reaching of all questions and presses for an answer. Is the infinite and eternal Essence, the Supreme Being, the omnipotent Power, an intelligent Essence, a rational Self, or is it merely an irrational entity, a blind force? It is clear that we could not adore a senseless Power, that we could not love a Being that lacks the attribute of reason. We might stand in awe and dread of the Universal Power. We might at times crouch in abject fear before the manifestation of its deadly terrors. We might use all possible means to avoid coming into conflict with the inexorable ways of the almighty and omnipresent Being, lest we be crushed by a blow dealt us by its outstretched arm. We might view with speechless wonder the multitudinous forms of inanimate and animate life which the infinite Being assumes. We might with eager curiosity try to discover the immutable laws which govern the universe from center to circumference. But we could not worship and venerate that Power. We could not bow our head in humility before the Infinite as being higher and better than man. For the highest and noblest kind of existence, is reason, the most divine reality is the knowing mind, the most worshipful power is the purposeful will realizing the ends of goodness.

If the Infinite is not a spiritual Power, we are shut up to materialism. The wings of faith are cut. We can not escape from the prison of self and commune in sorrow and joy with the general Soul.

Now what proof have we that intelligence is a quality of the universal Essence, that the all-generating, all-sustaining Power is a conscious Self? My answer is: The existence of thinking and willing beings on our planet, the existence of consciousness in each person, gives proof that the ground of all existence must be an intelligent Entity, that the almighty Power, of which our minds are manifestations, can not but be a rational Energy.

Let us full earnestly consider that kind of existence which we call Consciousness. What is consciousness? What a question, you will reply. Consciousness is consciousness. This is the only term by which it can be expressed. It is the only definition we can give it. Sensation, feeling, perception, thought, are names denoting various manifestations, simple or complex, of the same unique phenomenon of consciousness. It is absolutely unlike any form of material being, it has no quality in common with any kind of external existence. For this reason consciousness can be stated only to be what it is— consciousness; to be identical with itself only and to have no affinity with anything else.

But is it indeed impossible to compare mind with some physical reality, be it matter or force? Let us just try. All things material have three dimensions, length, breadth, and height. Suppose you ask, How long, how broad, how high is consciousness? Why, you will say, Not even a madman can conceive such a question. Right enough: Is consciousness thick or thin, hard or soft? Is it in a solid, liquid, or gaseous state? Leave us alone, you will cry, with your crazy questions! The attributes of extension and density do not apply to mind. Well, we take note of this self-evident fact and will soon make use of it in our argument. What is the color of consciousness? Is it white, black, red, green, or yellow? Is consciousness warm or cold, sweet or bitter? You exclaim, Stop putting to us such questions, which sound like the gibberish of madness. But your amazement, your vehement protests, simply make it as clear as noonday that none of the qualities of matter can be in thought ascribed to mind. Now, we know a thing, a being, exclusively by its qualities. Since mind and matter have so far been shown to have no quality in common, therefore they can not be compared with each other, they can not be placed in the same class. Consequently they can not be of the same essence and nature.

Again, consciousness can not be tasted nor smelled nor touched nor seen nor heard. The five senses have no access to it, they can not penetrate to it, receive impressions, combine them into qualities, and by such operations inform us what mind is. On the other hand, all we know of matter, of the world external to us, comes to us as a message of the senses. Without the senses matter of every kind and form would be absolutely unknown to us, the external world would simply have no existence for us. We would be wholly shut up within our self-consciousness. Again, we can not imagine consciousness to be identical with force, such as is manifested in the physical universe. We know force first of all and chiefly as motion appearing in moving bodies. Can you conceive consciousness as a sort of motion? I appeal to your own inward experience. Has feeling, willing, thinking, any feature in common with what we call motion, moving from place to place? Force under certain given conditions is changed from motion to heat. Can you realize in thought that consciousness is nothing but a form of heat? Well, force reveals itself also as electricity and magnetism. Is consciousness perhaps a species of electricity or magnetism? Try to think it out this very moment. Can you say to yourself: As I am observing my consciousness, I feel it to be like the electric currents in a battery or like the magnetic force? Why, your mind at once tells you, that identification is an unthinkable absurdity.

You have the direct and incontestable testimony of your mind that consciousness is absolutely unlike both matter and force. Yet consciousness undoubtedly exists. Your own self is consciousness. Your truest and inmost being is spirit or soul. Whence comes our consciousness? From what ground did consciousness spring? Our minds form part of the universal existence. It did not rise into being by itself and through itself. Our spirit must have its origin and existence in the universal existence. It can not be the offspring of matter and motion or force, because it is in every respect different from them. Only like begets its like. You can by no effort of imagination or thought bring yourself to realize that your mind is nothing but a species of matter or, what amounts to the same thing, a product of matter. You are absolutely unable to think of feeling and will as a peculiar form of heat, electricity, or motion. On this head Professor Huxley writes in his inimitable style: "It seems to me pretty plain, that there is a third thing in the universe, to wit, consciousness, which in the hardness of my heart and head I can not see to be matter, or force, or any conceivable modification of either, however intimately the manifestations of the phenomena of consciousness may be connected with the phenomena known as force."

Since consciousness can be derived from neither matter nor force, we are driven to the conclusion, that it must have its ground and origin in something which is like it, namely, in a superhuman consciousness or a universal mind. Human consciousness can not have sprung into existence out of nothing. For nothing will in all eternity bring forth nothing. We dare not say that mind has from eternity to eternity existed only as human consciousness, as spirit in man. For there was surely a time when the human race had as yet no existence. There was, beyond a doubt, a time, when the earth had not yet been formed and become a fit dwelling-place for rational beings. Mind must, therefore, have existed in the universe before the birth of animals and people on our globe. The conclusion is thus forced upon us that intelligence is an eternal reality. We can not say that it exists only as an isolated phenomenon in some parts of the universe and nowhere else. For the universal and infinite existence is one being and power, forever and everywhere identical with its own self; it would, therefore be the height of absurdity to ascribe consciousness to only a part of the Infinite, seeing that the Infinite consists of no separate parts but is an absolute, self-identical Unity, all whose manifestations are revelations of its hidden essence, and self-hood. The infinite and eternal Existence and Power, whom we call God, is thus shown to be a conscious Being or a universal Intelligence, the fountain-head of all consciousness in

finite existence. The conclusion of the matter, then:
The Eternal is a spiritual Being.

* * * * *

The argument has, however, not yet fully satisfied
you. Your doubts have not yet been completely
dispelled. The greatest of all difficulties is still
obstructing your path towards a rational belief in an
intelligent supreme Power. How can we possibly
believe in a universal mind-like Being? How can
mind exist without a nervous system, without a brain?
All mind-life, which we know of, appears in
connection with nerves, and the most highly-developed
intelligence is indissolubly bound up with the central
organ of the nervous system, the brain. If you destroy
a person's brain, their mind manifests its existence in
no manner whatever. Let a person's brain be seriously
injured, and they become a maniac or will sink into a
state of death-like sleep. When the heart ceases to
beat and no longer sends the current of vitalizing blood
to the brain, the body dies and with it the mind seems
to vanish into nothing. How, then, are we to believe
that the Supreme Being is a conscious entity? For the
blasphemous idea must of course be ruled out, that
there is somewhere in the world a gigantic divine brain
communicating with every part of the universe by
means of an all-pervading nervous system.

To minds not trained in philosophical thinking, to
minds not accustomed to rise above the analogies of
sense-experience, these objections appear fatal to the
belief in a conscious, absolute, and infinite Being.
They are the main considerations, why so many people
who implicitly trust their own rough and ready
judgments regarding what is possible or impossible,

have to their own hearts' grief come to imagine that they do not believe in God.

It is a mistake that the manifestations of feeling and will are absolutely dependent on that peculiar organization of matter called nerves. There are innumerable forms of exceedingly small animate beings, termed microbes, which do not show the faintest trace of nerves. They possess no organs internal and external of any kind. Yet these tiny structureless and nerveless creatures plainly exhibit the phenomena of feeling and willing. They pursue their prey, seize and devour it. They become aware of danger and try to escape from it. By such and similar actions they give unmistakable evidence of discerning and volitional impulses. These facts clearly prove that feeling and willing which are the web and woof of all mind-life can exist without any nervous apparatus. If nerves and brain were the absolute condition and ultimate cause of all mental phenomena, the existence of sentient creatures devoid of nerves and brain would be an utter impossibility. But you will object and say: "Those creatures lowest in the scale of animate life display but the dimmest and most shadowy beginnings of feeling and willing. All developed intelligence, all consciousness deserving that name, is invariably found in closest connection with a brain. The more highly developed a creature's brain, the greater is its mentality. Human intelligence is immeasurably superior to that of all other living beings, just because the human brain is more perfect, more finely organized than all others. If the world-ground is intelligent, it must be mind of the highest kind, infinitely superior to the human mind. But how can we reconcile the belief in a universal intelligence with the facts of experience which tell us that there is no consciousness without a brain?"

To this I reply: If the brain could ever be shown to explain the existence of consciousness, your reasoning would have some force. If science could ever demonstrate how matter organized as brain brings forth mind out of what is not itself mind there would be some show of reason for asserting that the brain is the parent cause of consciousness and hence that mental life is impossible where the assumed creative force is absent. But will the most minute and thorough knowledge of the structure and composition of the brain ever enable us to say: "We clearly see and observe how the brain manufactures thought. There is no longer any mystery about the origin and nature of mind"? Suppose we should even succeed in fixing upon the exact spot and the special cells of the brain in which each particular thought takes its rise. Suppose science should one day be able to make visible to the eye every wave and tremor in the brain substance accompanying every thought. Suppose physiology should one day bring into clear view the peculiar set of molecular and chemical changes which occur in the substances of the brain, while a certain set of ideas is passing through the mind. Still such knowledge would in no way explain the existence of consciousness. It would in no possible manner show how the molecules of matter making up the brain can produce mind which is absolutely unlike matter. For the brain is after all no more and no less than highly organized matter. Over eighty per cent of the brain substance is made up of the elements of hydrogen and oxygen, which, chemically combined, form water. Nitrogen, sulphur, carbon, iron, and other elements are the materials out of which an inscrutable Power has built the glorious dwelling of the mind, the brain. Now, we have shown that consciousness can not be identified with matter and motion, that it is impossible to conceive of mind as a modification or product of either. Matter in the form of brain still remains matter. It can not transcend its essence and quality and be changed from what matter is throughout the universe, and by virtue of organization give birth to mind. Since, then, the brain does not explain the existence of consciousness and can not be regarded as the generating source of mind, we have no right to hold that under no possible conditions can consciousness exist without a brain, and that consequently the infinite ground of being can not be believed to be intelligent. All that we may say is that under the given terrestrial conditions, as far as we know, intelligence of the higher kind invariably appears in closest connection and interaction with a brain, that the finite human mind, while incarnate in a body, manifests itself through the agency of a complete nervous system centered in a brain. But our sense-bound experience does not justify us in laying it down as a universal and absolute law that it is impossible for mind to exist outside of a brain.

Our experience alone does not suffice to decide with incontrovertible certainty what is possible and what is impossible. How shall we determine that something is absolutely impossible? Innumerable things for ages have been universally believed to be impossible which a larger experience has proved to be possible. To talk and be heard at a distance of thousands of miles, but a few years ago seemed impossible. Yet the telephone has now made it possible. To catch the dread force of electricity, to make it carry a person's message from one end of the earth to the other with incredible swiftness, to harness lightning like a horse to our wagon, to make it light up our houses and streets, to heat up our dwellings and cook our meals, until recent times was deemed utterly impossible. In the time of Columbus no human being considered it possible to cross the Atlantic in iron ships in less than six days without the use of sails. In biblical times it was held impossible to measure the earth and weigh it in balances. In our days the length, height, and depth, the weight and density of the sun, moon, and every planet are perfectly well known. Spectroscopy has in our days made possible what two centuries ago was regarded as a self-evident impossibility. The human mind can nowadays ascertain with scientific exactness the number and nature of the atomic elements present not only in our sun but in the remotest stars, whose light travels six thousand years before reaching our globe. The idea of changing air into a liquid and even turning it into a solid until recent times was denied by the strongest evidence of experience. Yet the testimony of experience, so long accepted with unquestioning faith by all people, in these days of ours has proved to be fallacious. According to the data of our given experience it is impossible to transform coal, stones, and other materials into food for people and animals. Yet the science of chemistry, which is still in its infancy, will probably one day be able to change inorganic matter into organic means of subsistence. Countless other things which are now universally believed to be beyond the range of possibility, one day will come to be well-known realities exciting as little surprise as the telegraph and telephone.

What, then, is eternally and absolutely impossible?' That which is absolutely unthinkable, which is an irreconcilable contradiction to the indestructible categories of our mind. That is *a priori* impossible which is at war with the inborn ideas of the soul. The most fundamental of these innate ideas is: It is impossible for anything to spring from nothing. The law of universal causality, the necessary belief that nothing can exist or happen without a sufficient cause, is but another expression of the same innate idea. Hence, it is an absolute impossibility that matter in any imaginable form, matter in the guise of nerve and brain, should be the parent cause of mind. Matter having no quality whatever in common with thought, the rise of consciousness out of it would be a new creation out of nothing, which is unthinkable.

Still both matter and mind exist. Neither can be identified with the other, nor can they be derived from each other. The two worlds, the inner world of consciousness and the external world of objects, seem to fall apart. In spite of their intimate relations and interactions these two eternal forms of existence seem separated by a yawning chasm with no bridge leading from one to the other. They face each other as irreconcilable contrasts. Materialism can by no tricks of sophistical reasoning drive mind from its position as a self-existing entity. Idealism can not deny matter and prove it to be a mere illusion. But the human mind can not rest in such dualism. The soul finds no peace in a world divided in itself. The very root of all knowledge is the indestructible and immediate belief that the universe forms a unity, that the soul is co-related to the world in all its parts, that all being is of one source, of one essence, of one energy. The very ground of all knowledge is the innate belief that behind the inner world of consciousness, and behind the phenomena of the world of objects, there is Divine

Unity in which they are both embraced and in which their differences are reconciled and disappear. This belief in an all-pervading and all-enfolding Unity which binds together matter and mind in a supreme harmony, underlies all thought. This one Being reveals Itself as nature, and manifests Itself and is present in us as mind. In this all-enfolding Unity we live, move, and have our being. Yet this Unity transcends both the human mind and nature. It is infinite and absolute. It is not circumscribed by the conditions within which matter exists. It is not circumscribed by the limitations which bound our intelligence.

This essay was originally published in slightly different form in July 1895.

CHAPTER 3

Yahvism

AMONG the innumerable misfortunes which have befallen the Israelites since they ceased to form a state and a nation, one of the most fatal in its consequences is the name Judaism. In the mind of the Gentiles this name indissolubly associates our religion, which is universal in its deepest sources and universal in its scope and tendency, with the Jewish race, and thus stamps it as a tribal religion. Worse still, the Jews themselves, who have gradually come to call their religion Judaism, are most of them misled to believe that their faith is bound up altogether with the Jewish race, that it is a religion for Jews alone and not for people of any other race or nationality.

Yet, neither in biblical nor in post-biblical, neither in Talmudic nor in much later times, is the term Judaism ever heard of among the Israelites. The Bible speaks of the religion of Israel as "Torath Yahve", the instruction, or the moral law, revealed by Yahweh; more fully it is stated to be the statutes, judgments, and ordinances of Yahweh. In other places, what we are wont to call the religion of Israel is represented as "Yirath Yahve", the fear and reverence of Yahweh. These and other kindred appellations continued for many ages to stand for the religion of Israel among its adherents. To distinguish it from Christianity and Islam, the Jewish philosophers sometimes designate it as the faith or the belief of the Jews. It was Flavius Josephus, writing for the instruction of Greeks and Romans, who coined the term Judaism, in order to pit it against Hellenism as a worthy opponent and rival. By Hellenism was understood the civilization, comprising language, poetry, religion, art, science, manners, customs, and institutions, which, since the times of Alexander, had spread from Greece, its original home, over vast regions of Europe, Asia, and Africa. Josephus, zealous for the glory of his nation, wished to prove to his pagan contemporaries that the Jewish conceptions of God, of the soul, of morality, enshrined in a noble literature, were in most respects superior to those of Hellenism. And to the totality of their beliefs, moral commandments, religious practices, and ceremonial institutions he gave the name of Judaism. The Christian writers eagerly seized upon the name thus furnished them, in order to distinguish Christianity from the mother-religion from which it had sprung and become differentiated; they were thus enabled to demonstrate to the heathens, who were seeking the true God, that for them to embrace the religion of Israel meant to become Jews, members of the hated, despised, and already persecuted Jewish race. Moreover, the Jews themselves, who intensely detested the traitor Josephus, refrained from reading his works and from adopting any of his theological, practical, or historical ideas. Hence, the term Judaism coined by Josephus remained absolutely unknown to them. It was only in comparatively recent times, after the Jews became familiar with modern Christian literature, that they began to name their religion Judaism.

But why object to this name and try to supplant it by another, if it does most fitly express the facts, the whole of those religious ideas and practices for which it stands? Is it not really the religion of Jews and of no other race besides? Has not your religion, an inquiring Christian may ask, from its dim beginnings to this day, exclusively and jealously been confined to the so-called *chosen people,* the lineal descendants of Abraham, Isaac, and Jacob? When did the Jews ever bring the light and truth of their religion, the moral ideas and laws in which it glories, to people of other races and nationalities? To these questions I will reply, not with the fencing logic of an advocate arguing for one side of a case, but from the depths of my religious convictions: A religion, which has moral monotheism for its basis, the belief in one only God, the Maker of heaven and earth, a religion which teaches that all people are descended from one first father and mother, and, hence, that all people, without distinction of race or climate, are made like their first parents in the image and likeness of God; a faith which proclaims that God is the author, sustainer, law-giver, and judge of all people, can not be tribal and national, can not reserve all its store of light and moral truths for one people alone, to the exclusion of all other races, leaving the rest of the world forever to grope in darkness, and to perish in corruption through ignorance of the right way. Such a religion is bound to be universal in its extent; it must strive, unless it belie its very motive, to bring its good tidings to all people, it must put forth efforts to bestow the blessings of which it is in possession upon all the families of the earth, to educate all the peoples according to the truths it holds, to teach them the ways of righteousness and holiness in which they should go. A tribal or national religion, one that does not cherish the desire to extend its empire beyond the limits of a certain race or people, is essentially a pagan religion, at least it has not yet rid itself of certain ideas which are characteristic of Paganism.

What is the cardinal difference between Paganism and the religion of Israel, or Monotheism? Every nation in antiquity had a supreme god of its own, from whom it believed itself descended through mythical ancestors. Every national god cared only for the welfare of that god's own people, being utterly indifferent to the material and spiritual interests of other nations, simply because they were not that god's children and stood in no relation to that god. Each god loved only its own nation, and was relentlessly hostile to those nations that were at war with its people. The children of a god's nation were bound to obey that god's voice, to fulfill that god's commands and ordinances, to seek that god's favor, and to show their gratitude to that god for its protection. The glory of one's nation was also the glory of the national god, its defeat was the god's defeat. With the disappearance of the people, that people's god lost its empire, and vanished into nothingness.

The religion of Israel arose in irreconcilable opposition to this pagan theology. Yahweh, God who was, is, and will be, is the God of heaven and earth, the ruler of all nations. All people are Yahweh's children, because they are stamped with Yahweh's spiritual likeness, because they derive their life from the breath of life which Yahweh has breathed into them. Yahweh is the Sovereign of the spirits of all flesh. Yahweh's divine laws of justice are binding on all people, for Yahweh is the judge of the whole earth. Yahweh visits their transgressions on all nations. Yahweh's mercy is extended over all creatures, and Yahweh graciously pardons the sins of repentant heathens, that heed the warnings of Yahweh's prophets, and return from their evil ways. Israel is not Yahweh's sole possession. From the rising of the sun to its setting is Yahweh's name to be praised among the nations. Abraham, who sought the true God, and found Yahweh, was chosen to be a blessing to all people, and through his seed should all families of the earth be blessed. Israel was chosen to be the light-bearer of God's truth, God's missionary to teach the nations the knowledge of God, and show them the way in which they should walk. The children of Israel were not to enjoy special privileges and favors, but were to be witnesses of Yahweh. Israel is the servant of God that will not grow faint nor become weary until Yahweh has established justice on earth. The servants of God suffer for the sins of the nations, are despised and their visage is not like that of a person, their voices are not raised on high, even the bruised reed do they not break. Laden with sorrows, bleeding from many wounds, the servant is ordained to gather the lost sheep, the nations of the earth, unto Yahweh, their Parent and Judge.

Such is the ideal mission of Israel, as conceived by the seers of Yahweh. Nor has the historic life of Israel in its better days, whenever the conditions of the time favored such a course, been faithless to its high universal mission. The best writers in Israel had a more or less clear insight into the fact that Israel had not been formed into a people by race affinities, but by the formative and unifying forces of spiritual kinship. It was early recognized that Israel was not what is called a pure race, but had received large accretions from foreign tribes. Judah, the reputed father of the tribe of Judah, we are informed, married a Canaanite woman who gave birth to the ancestors of the Jewish clans. This simply signifies that the tribe of Judah grew out of a union of Israelite and Canaanite tribes. In fact, the Calebites, the Yerachmeelites, and the Kenizites, though forming integral parts of Judah, even in later historic times were known to have been of Canaanite origin. Joseph married Osnath, an Egyptian, or, translated into the language of history, the tribes of Ephraim and Manasseh received large Egyptian accretions. A whole clan of Simeon was called Saul, the son of the Canaanite woman, which means that it contained so many native elements that it was looked upon as largely Canaanite. Moses married a Midianite woman, and his children were therefore of mixed blood. The whole Midianite clan, into which Moses married, was adopted into the Israelite nation, and played an important part in the religious history of Israel. It is agreed on all hands that the great mass of the indigenous population of Canaan were gradually absorbed by the Israelites, and their blood blended with that of the conquerors. The ancestress of the sacred dynasty of David was Ruth, a daughter of the hated Moabite people. Already during the Babylonian captivity many converts were made to the religion of Israel, as is evidenced by the fact that numerous families were found among the returned exiles, unable to prove that they were of Israelite descent. The prophet Deutero-Isaiah welcomes the strangers, who join themselves to Yahweh, to serve God. Of them

God will take to minister in God's Temple. Several centuries later large regions of Babylonia were inhabited by native Babylonians, who had become converted to the religion of Israel. The royal family of Adiabene and many great nobles were proselytes and proved themselves most generous to their co-religionists in times of misfortune. During the last century of the Second Commonwealth the religion of Israel was gaining millions of converts. There was hardly a city in the Roman Empire which had not an Israelite congregation largely composed of converts from the Pagan religions. At the time of Paul almost all the women in Damascus had embraced Judaism. The Pharisees, the most zealous, the most numerous and progressive sect of Israel, are accused by the Gospel writers of traversing wide seas and lands to make a convert. Still later, in the ninth century CE, a rabbi converted the royal family of the Khazaars, the whole nobility, and a large part of the common people to his religion. Proselytes were always held in high esteem by the Israelites. It was not until Christianity, having ascended the throne, forbade the Jews, on pain of death, to make or receive converts that the proselytizing zeal of Israel was checked. Those who read the history of Israel with an impartial mind must be convinced that the leading and most enlightened minds aspired to make the religion of Yahweh the religion of mankind.

But it shall not be denied that there were other tendencies and forces at work opposed to the universal aspirations of our religion. There occur numerous passages in the Bible, mostly, however, in the historical, not in the prophetic parts, which do not breathe this lofty universal spirit, but betray a spirit of national exclusiveness. We must, however, judge a religion and the literature in which it is embalmed by its highest manifestations. We must go to the root-principles of every religion, to its creative elements, and then consider whatsoever agrees with them as vital and permanent, and whatsoever contradicts them as a passing phase, as a temporary aberration, caused by the pressure of deteriorating, adverse circumstances. The chief cause in checking the universal tendency of Yahvism, was the ever-present fear that by coming in close contact with the surrounding nations the Israelites would learn their ways and practice their abominations, and, instead of leading people to the true God, would themselves be misled to worship idols and defile themselves with the shameless iniquities of idolatry.

Of such infinite importance was the worship of Yahweh and the knowledge of Yahweh's ways held to be, so great and imminent seemed the danger that the light of revelation, but dimly burning in the heart of the Israelite masses, might be totally extinguished by the dense darkness of the pagan world, that many writers and law-givers wished to isolate Israel, in order to preserve in its midst the world's priceless blessings. Hence, those utterances and enactments, born of a spirit of exclusiveness, which stand in such glaring contrast with the spirit of universality of the great prophets and with the cardinal ideas of Yahvism. Moreover, Israel, though ideally the chosen messenger of Yahweh to all nations, under the given actual conditions formed a people and a state, struggling for independence and often for its existence, surrounded on all sides by hostile nations that sought to subjugate it, and even to destroy its name from the face of the earth. A state of mutual hostility does not tend to awaken feelings of amity, to foster the ideas of universal commonwealth. Yet, in spite of all these tremendous difficulties, the spirit of universality, the belief in the unity of God and the unity of mankind, was forcing its way into the foreground of the national consciousness. In the leading minds, at least, this spirit gained the supremacy over all contending interests and ideas, and especially after the great triumph of Yahvism under the Maccabees it sought ways and means to realize itself.

But there was an obstacle in the way of its realization far more formidable than all the opposing forces mentioned above. Many causes, which can not be enumerated here, had concurred to develop the ceremonial laws to stupendous dimensions. The Jews alone, who had *gradually,* in a long course of historic training, grown into them, could make the serious attempt to shape their life in accordance with them without feeling them as a burden. The rest of the world, especially the Western peoples, regarded these countless strict ordinances and ceremonies as unnatural and insupportable burdens. These ceremonies formed a wall of separation between the world and Israel. The wonder is that the spirit of Yahvisin succeeded in making so many converts in spite of being grievously hampered in its march by the weight of the ceremonial yoke. Christianity sprang into existence and started on its career with the intense strength of, and with the ardent enthusiasm for, Israel's mission to the nations. Freed from the trammels of ceremonial law by Paul, at once it gained an immense advantage over the Mother-church, which dared not break away from its peculiar national forms. This was the tragedy of Israel, that it had within itself a universal soul and a national soul, each contending for the mastery and neither able to obtain it. During the Middle Ages there was no possibility for Yahvism to spread within the domain of Christendom. The penalty for making converts was torture and death. Thus Yahvism was surrounded within by a high wall made of hard, firmly-cemented ceremonies and without by the dreadful wall of fanaticism, hatred, and suspicion.

How could pure Yahvism dream of making conquests? Yet the belief in a Messiah to come implied not only the future deliverance of the Jews from the world's hatred and cruel persecution, but also the assurance of the reign of universal peace and universal commonwealth under the sway of Yahweh, the God proclaimed by Israel. But it was a mere dream, a far-off vision which had no feature common with any possible reality. For the first time in many centuries an arena has been opened in this country, and in our age, for pure Yahvism to unfold its universal nature, to accomplish its mission as a religion of many races and nations, to gather into its folds those Gentiles, whose reason can not accept the peculiar tenets of Christianity, who are separated from us only by a name.

The Israelites of America, at least the overwhelming majority of the enlightened, the truly genuine American Israelites, have completely emancipated themselves from the yoke of ceremonial laws, have broken down the inner wall, built by the hand of Talmudic and later times, which has kept Jews and Gentiles apart. True, the outer wall, raised by prejudice, ignorance, race antipathies, and religious fanaticism, though many breaches have been made in it, is still far from being demolished. But let us at least do our part to the best of our ability; let us try to perform the task which the God of History has

imposed upon us; let us remove every obstacle from
the way in which the universal spirit of Yahvism would
move, and as a first important step let us give up the
name Judaism, which is a hindrance to the spread of
our religion. Painful though the truth be, let us not
hide it from ourselves, that many who would embrace
our faith, because they are already as one with us in
belief, refrain from doing so because they do not wish
to become Jews, because by embracing Judaism they
believe they lose their own race and nationality and
become adopted into the Jewish nation and race. Let
us call our religion YAHVISM. It is no new-fangled
name, it is simply the name by which our faith was
called and cherished by our forefathers, who
designated it as YIRATH YAHVE, the religion of
Yahweh. It is the fittest of all possible names for our
religion. It is the expression of our cardinal beliefs
and the profoundest ideas of our faith. Under this
name we adore God as Eternal and Infinite Existence,
as the source of all being. As Yahweh we worship God
as Omniscient Providence. Yahweh is the Creator, the
Preserver and Ruler of nature and humanity. Yahweh
is our Sovereign, is our Law-giver, our Judge and
Savior. As Yahweh God was revealed to Moses, the
founder of our religion. As soon as we shall be
accustomed to name and proclaim our religion as
Yahvism and to call its adherents Yahvists, it will be
set free to begin once more its predestined career of
conquest. Many Gentiles who now shrink from
religious fellowship with us, though at heart our co-
religionists, because they do not wish to become Jews
by embracing Judaism, will readily flock to the banner
of Yahvism, will gladly call themselves by the name of
Yahweh, will proudly proclaim themselves Yahvists.
Many again, who now claim kinship with us by virtue

of Jewish parentage, although they have turned their backs upon our religion, despising its truths and mission, will cease to be regarded as members of our community as soon as our religion, by assuming the name of Yahvism, will be dissociated in thought from the Jewish race. There is a tremendous, a magic power in a name! With a name you may keep alive the demons of contempt, of race-prejudice, of historical hatred; with a name you may conjure up the angel of mutual respect, of union, and universal love.

This essay was originally published in slightly different form in June 1894.

CHAPTER 4

Ceremonialism

THE Jews of today, who live in the most advanced
countries of the world, are, with every fiber of their
being, part and parcel of modern civilization. At the
same time they know themselves to be the heirs of the
ancient national religion of the Hebrew people and the
foreordained continuators of the spiritual history and
mission of Israel.

This twofold life of the modern Jew on the one hand
is a high privilege and a source of spiritual power, and
on the other it brings on numerous conflicts, some of
which appear irreconcilable. The customs, usages,
and ceremonial laws of the ancient Asiatic Hebrews
and of the isolated medieval Jews are in many respects
hopelessly antagonistic to the ways of life of modern
Western civilization. Let us not in a spirit of levity
and self-delusion slur over this fact. Let us full
earnestly face it, as becomes sincere people. We may
deny it with our lips, but in our heart abides the
conviction that the contrast is there, often glaring,

between the old and the new order of things, between Canaan and Europe. We are the children of two worlds; with heart and soul we belong to both, and only with the last breath would we renounce either of them.

It is true the Christians are also very largely Israelitish in sentiment, belief, and ethics. Our Book of Life is also their Book of Books. The lofty moral ideals, which were evolved during post-biblical times, and which in many respects mark a considerable advance beyond those of the Bible, are also embodied in the writings of the New Testament. Our prophets and sweet singers, our heroes and martyrs, are also venerated by the Christians and looked up to as noble types of God-seeking humanity. But Christianity, though at first a national Jewish sect, soon spread westward, from Asia to Europe, from the Jews to the Greeks and Romans, and became in the course of a century or two thoroughly denationalized. In its struggle for existence, growth, and expansion Christianity broke loose from almost all distinctively national customs, ceremonies, and laws which were repugnant and unacceptable to the Western peoples. Through this act of denationalization, the abolition of all ancestral usages and regulations which had no moral meaning and educational purpose for the world at large, Christianity got the start of Judaism in the conversion of humanity. Without this bold departure it would have continued through, perhaps, four or five generations as an insignificant Jewish sect, at last to disappear and be forgotten. By casting off the garb of national ceremonialism Christianity succeeded in becoming one of the great universal religions.

The rise and spread of Islam, which almost extirpated the Christian religion in the East, caused

the latter to be thenceforth for good and evil identified
with the life and history of the Western nations.
During the Middle Ages Christianity came to be
tainted with the fierce and gloomy superstitions,
inoculated with the savage instincts of the new
barbarous nations inhabiting Europe, corrupted with
the gross vices of the primitive Teutons and Slavs, and
contaminated with the more refined immoralities of the
Latin and Greek races. With the resurrection of the
sciences and arts and the rebirth of the Israelite moral
powers, it emerges along with the Western nations
from a state of seeming decadence and degeneracy to
new purity and vigor. If it did not lead, it at least
followed steadily in the wake of advancing Western
civilization, for the simple and cogent reason that the
Western nations, that are the creators and standard-
bearers of modern culture, happen to be also the
highest representatives and acknowledged standard-
bearers of Christianity. True it is, the results of
modern science and the theory of the universe it holds,
in more than one respect seem to clash with some of
the vital dogmas, and to negate some of the essential
doctrines, of the Christian religion as authoritatively
taught by the Catholic and the Protestant churches.
But these grave questions concern merely matters of
faith and philosophy. As to manners and customs and
the general ways of life there practically exists no
antagonism between Western Christianity and Western
civilization. The antagonism, as has been said, is
confined to problems of metaphysics and to differences
between ideal ethics and actual imperfect conduct.

When we turn from Christianity to the
contemplation of Judaism in its relation to modern
civilization, we are met with difficulties of a different
nature; one might say with difficulties of an opposite

kind. In matters of faith and dogma Judaism finds itself in full accord with the general postulates of modern science. It knows of but one theory of the universe which it is bound to combat to the bitter end, namely, soulless materialism or atheism. In the holy of holies of religious metaphysics the central ideas of Judaism dwell in peace and conscious harmony with the boldest and most comprehensive conception of modern Western philosophy. The belief in the absolute unity of God, implying the unity of universal life; the belief that unbounded nature is a perennial and progressive manifestation of the creative Infinite; the belief that justice and love are not accidental phenomena appearing in humanity, but are the divine revelations of the perfection and mercy of the Eternal; the doctrine that the human soul is godlike in essence and dignity and free from the taint of any imaginary hereditary guilt or curse; the conviction that each person is a free moral agent, dependent for good or evil, for self-mastery or self-degradation, on their own free will; the view that there is a Messianic future in store for humanity, when there will be a perfect humanity spontaneously living according to the indwelling laws of God: these vital tenets of Judaism, professed by all its adherents, by orthodox and reformer, are the very ideas which the greatest and profoundest philosophers of Europe have presented and are presenting as the last outcome and the most precious fruits of their speculation! The Ark of the Covenant, subsisting between God and humanity, containing the everlasting laws of justice and love, rests safely within the sanctuary of Israel's religion. No iconoclastic hands will ever break it. It will endure as long as the heavens endure. Philosophy and science are the cherubim from between whose wings the still divine voice speaks from the mercy-seat of the human heart and mind! In matters of faith and ethics Judaism has indeed anticipated, or held pace with, the intellectual and moral progress of the most advanced civilization. But when we consider the outward forms and the ceremonial garb of Judaism, its most enthusiastic votaries can not close their eyes to the fact that it has here and elsewhere, but more especially in European lauds, very much to throw aside entirely, much to change and modify, in order to be perfectly at one with the ways of life of modern civilization, so as to become in the deepest and widest sense one of its living and universal spiritual powers. With the exception of the numerous reform congregations in America, Judaism is still wearing, even in the most advanced countries of Europe, the ceremonial garments which fitted it well enough in Asia, but which look strange, out of date, and out of fit in the midst of the Western nations of today. Though universal to the core, though necessarily universal in tendency, though knowing itself destined by Providence to gather into its fold many millions from all nations, it yet appears to the eye of the fairest observers clad in its antiquated ceremonial costume which distinguished it during the grievous isolation of the Middle Ages. Millions and tens of millions of Gentiles who are no longer Christians even in name, but are at one with us in all the essential elements of our religion, feel themselves repelled from Judaism. For, by retaining all its national ceremonies, usages, and laws dating from biblical, Talmudic, and medieval times, it is made to appear intensely national or tribal, narrow and exclusive, and strangely out of harmony with its Western surroundings.

The student of history full well knows why Judaism has thus in *seeming* remained national and outlandish. Like all ancient religions, the religion of Israel was national in origin and scope. It had its roots deep in the heart of the people, it grew out of the spiritual experience of the people, it derived its purest and strongest forces from the vigorous morality of the chosen people; it was bound up with all the forms, customs, and laws of the national life; it was in keeping with the climate, and adjusted to the habits, manners, and occupations of that agricultural race; it was intertwined with all the historical memories of Israel, joyful and mournful. True, the greatest and wisest of God's prophets, in whom God's spirit was a lamp shining far into futurity, in whose soul the indestructible essence of Israel's religion, ethical monotheism, blossomed forth into the ideas and ideals of universal love and universal humanity, these wondrous seers in their boldest visions often broke through the bounds of nationality, declaring in accents still ringing through the ages that Yahweh was the God and Parent, not of Israel alone, but of all the nations of the earth, and that Yahweh's laws of justice and mercy will one day come to be the laws of life to all the tribes of humanity. They decried many ancient ways and ancestral usages dear to the people's heart as vicious and ungodly. They sneered at most of the inherited religious practices and ceremonies, thought by the priesthood and the populace to constitute true piety. Even the institution of sacrifices, which in the opinion of all ancient races was the very essence and life of religion, was held in abhorrence by the foremost of Israel's prophets. The greatest of them all proclaims in the name of Yahweh: "What is to me the multitude of your sacrifices? In the blood of bullocks and of lambs and of goats I have no delight. Bring no more false oblations! Incense is an abomination to me. Put away your evil doings from before mine eyes; cease to do evil, learn to do well; seek justice; relieve the oppressed; defend the defenseless; plead for those who have no one to plead for them." Micah has for all the families of the earth and for all the ages to come defined the true nature of religion in these memorable words: "Wherewith shall I come before the Eternal and bow myself before the most high God? Shall I come before God with burnt offerings, with calves of a year old? Will the Eternal be pleased with thousands of rams, or with ten thousands of rivers of oil? Shall I give my first-born for the sin of my soul, the fruit of my body for my transgression? God has showed thee, O people, what is good; what does Yahweh require of thee but to do justly, to love mercy, and to walk humbly before thy God?" Such were the religious ideas and moral ideals of Israel's best, of God's own chosen messengers. But the nation as a whole was not yet ripe for so lofty a religion. It was simply a psychological impossibility for the mass of the people to break away from most of its national conceptions and usages and rise to the dizzy heights of the prophet's universal religion of justice, mercy, and love of God! Had not Israel been providentially shattered to pieces and scattered abroad, had not the nation as a body been destroyed and only a remnant thereof been carried away from its native soil into captivity, it is not improbable that the national polytheistic elements, acting with the unbroken force of hereditary habits of thought and modes of action, would at last have overwhelmed the prophetic spirit of a purely moral monotheism. As it was, a remnant of the remnant was saved and rejuvenated by imbuing itself largely with the ideas, hopes, and aspirations of the prophets. Polytheism, together with all its abominations, was cast out from their heart and life, and ethical monotheism was firmly and forever established in their soul. They formed the nucleus of a new religious community, destined to be the leaven of humanity.

But could that fragment of the nation, concentrating as it did within itself the best and most vital spiritual forces of the past, help cherishing along with the glorious memories of the past also the hope of returning to the home of the fathers and there build up anew the old nationality on the foundations of the divine law? About fifty thousand devoted people, among them numerous priests, returned to Palestine and, amid ruins and desolation, began the arduous task of creating a new commonwealth on the basis of Israel's religion according to the laws, statutes, and ordinances of Yahweh. But which forms of the ancestral life were to be discarded and which retained? All those ceremonies and customs which were opposed to the spirit of monotheism were wholly done away with. On the other hand, all those modes of worship and forms of life which contained an element of morality or tended to bind the people together and distinguish it from the surrounding heathen tribes, were fondly preserved and embodied in the code of religious and national laws. The Temple was rebuilt and became the rallying center and the emblem of the national existence. Daily sacrifices were instituted anew and the priesthood, the children of Zadoc, the sole remaining representatives of the ancient ruling families, came to be invested with the supreme guiding power. The priests in course of time learned to consider themselves better and holier and nearer to God than the people, because they ministered in the temple of God, offering daily sacrifices to God and burning incense in the sanctuary, because they ate the sacred bread and meat of God, observing certain laws of Levitical purity and diet. Then rose a noble democratic spirit in Israel in opposition to the priestly claim to special sanctity. Great and wise teachers sprung from the mass of the people, proclaimed the doctrine that the whole people is holy, that God is in it and with it no less than in the children of Aaron; in a word, that all Israel was to be a kingdom of priests and a holy nation. To carry this grandly democratic idea into practice they extended the laws of Levitical purity and diet and, in part, also costume, to the whole mass of the people. All Jews should abstain from eating what was forbidden to the priests; the meat that came upon their table should be of an animal killed in the way the sacrifices were slain. Every person should wash their hands before breaking bread, just as the priest did before eating of the holy bread. What was impure to the children of Aaron should be equally impure to the children of the common people; what contaminated a priest should be considered polluting also to the body of every other Israelite. In these and in innumerable other respects all laypeople were made to observe with the most scrupulous care all the rules and laws which regulated the daily life of the priests. The effect of this religious policy was in many ways highly beneficial. It imbued the whole people with the consciousness of its priestly dignity and mission. It made every Jew feel that, as to sanctity, devotion, and godliness, they might be the peer of the high priest. Moreover, it fostered habits of cleanliness, temperance, and self-mastery.

But, as does frequently happen in the life of individuals and nations, in the pursuit of means to reach certain ends the latter are often lost sight of and the temporary means come to be treated as ultimate ends. The democratization of Judaism by means of popularizing the ceremonial laws was to serve the high purpose, first to make the whole nation a commonwealth of genuine priests of God, and then, through the agency of this elevated and humanized people, to impart the blessing of Israel's ethical monotheism, the statutes of justice and mercy, to all the families of the earth. The ceremonial laws gradually became so numerous, all-embracing, exacting, and burdensome that a very large portion of the Jewish nation itself, the so-called people of the land, was unable to live up to them, because it could not live under them. Thus there was an ever-widening gulf between the great mass of the uneducated, consisting mostly of peasants, and the learned classes, mostly inhabitants of the cities. Again, the ceremonial laws had gradually built up a perfect wall around Judaism, and prevented the pagan seeking the God of Israel from entering God's sanctuary except through the narrow ceremonial gate left open. Even under these immense difficulties and restrictions numerous Gentiles adopted Judaism and took upon themselves the whole burden of its laws. There was the spectacle of a lofty and thoroughly humane religion, which in its very nature and tendency was destined to become universal, yet which, through the concurrence of many historical influences, had become imprisoned within a thick shell of national laws and ceremonies, so that it could not go forth as the messenger of God to conquer the earth by the might of its divine moral powers. May be that if the fatal crisis had not so soon arrived, if the terrible struggle with murderous Rome had not cut the nation to pieces and laid waste Judaism's center of gravity, the process of historical development would have brought on a peaceful or revolutionary solution of the conflict between the universal soul and the ceremonial tribal body of Israel's religion. As it was, the fearful catastrophe, which had more than decimated the Jews and drained nearly all the life-blood of the nation, left Judaism prostrate and sick at heart, even nigh unto death. For a long time it could not think of spiritual conquest abroad. All that the leaders of Israel could do was to gather together and unite the scattered fragments and breathe into them the spirit of trust in God, of indomitable endurance, and of hope in a glorious future and mission.

Under such critical conditions, during the supreme struggle for mere existence, any attempt to dissolve the national ceremonial laws would have proved sure death both to the Jews and to Judaism. Meanwhile Christianity, untrammeled by national memories, disasters, and laws, was reaping the rich harvest prepared by the parent religion. Then came the ages of Christian dominance and supremacy, but, alas, also of Christian fanaticism. Then was ushered in the sad time when the Jews were driven back upon themselves, ostracized, calumniated, hunted down like wild beasts, robbed of all human rights, and shut up in narrow ghettos. No wonder that the poor, down-trodden exiles, the memories of whose past was their only solace, whose literature, Biblical and Talmudic, was their only home, whose hope in a Messianic deliverance was their only star in the night of misery, considered themselves an alien nation dwelling for a time among hostile nations, but destined one day to be restored to its sacred soil, to see Jerusalem rebuilt in all her glory, and the Temple of God erected anew, where sacrifices would as of yore be offered daily to the Most High. No wonder, since the present was dark as the darkness of Egypt, that our fathers turned their eye now back to the transfigured past and now lovingly towards the hoped-for national future. No wonder that they clung not only to the moral laws, but with equal devotion to all the ceremonial ordinances and statutes of Bible and Talmud, unconcerned with the question whether any of them had outgrown their time, meaning, and usefulness. Thus it came to pass, that not only were all the old ceremonial laws preserved and observed, as if they were imperishable, divinely-revealed moral laws, but innumerable new enactments and observances were year by year deduced from the older ones, often by means of hair-splitting casuistry. Ceremonial burden was heaped upon burden, restriction upon restriction, fence added to fence, until almost every step was hampered and every act hedged in by ceremony. The whole life of the Jews was enveloped with the ceremonial laws as with a huge spider's web.

At last, however, the light of tolerance has appeared. Civilization has tamed the dragon of fanaticism, broken down the walls of the ghettos, and with gracious words proclaimed to the Jews: "Go forth from your prison, breathe the air of liberty and equality, mingle with your brethren, live with them as the children of the same Parent, work with them and for them, let your spiritual light, which has so long burned in your dark prison, shine in the midst of humanity, contribute your share of intellectual, moral, religious, and artistic work to the store of the world's possessions." We have heard that divine voice of saving and liberating civilization, and have with grateful and joyful hearts leaped forth from the prison of isolation into the arena of modern life. We no longer feel ourselves an alien race dwelling in misery among hostile races. We know that we are flesh of the flesh, bone of the bone, and spirit of the spirit of Western civilization. We no longer are a nation within a nation, we no longer hope nor wish to be restored to Canaan and there begin a new national life. We are here to stay forever, to be with heart and soul and might children of Western civilization. We hope for no Messiah, but believe in the coming of the great day when there will be perfect humanity living in god-like harmony and union beneath the scepter of universal righteousness and love. We believe that we, the professors of Judaism, have still the sacred mission to hasten the great day of the Sovereign God by living according to the moral ideals of pure Judaism and to gather in those many Gentiles whose spirit urges them to walk with us in the ways of the prophets and sages of Israel.

Yet such a consummation, which is devoutly to be wished for, requires the most complete adaptation of Judaism to the views and habits of modern civilization. The inexorable spirit of history leaves us no other choice. The conditions of modern life and the exigencies of the times have in fact already decided the issue in a manner not to be mistaken or reversed. The overwhelming majority of the Jews living in the civilized countries of the world, and more especially the American Israelites, have virtually emancipated themselves from all such Mosaic and rabbinical laws as regulate diet, priestly purity, and dress. Even among those styling themselves "Orthodox" in this country there is not one in ten who strictly conforms to all the ceremonial laws as laid down in the Bible, the Talmud, and later authoritative books. There is not one in fifty among the German and native Orthodox

Jews in the United States who, under the genuine and unadulterated Jewish orthodoxy of Poland and Russia, does not deserve scourging and worse punishments in accordance with indisputable enactments, biblical or rabbinical. The truth of the matter is, the practice has long ago outrun the theory; or rather, it has pursued its own way without any theory, being blindly determined by social agencies at work. No protest, no grievous lamentation will ever bring to life what has irrevocably gone out of existence for want of harmony with its present environments.

But this very state of things gives much concern to those having the mission of Judaism greatly at heart. This rapid change, the speedy abolition of time-honored and immemorial forms and ceremonies, brought about by no clearly-conceived principle, but by mere stress of unconscious forces, has been and is fraught with great spiritual danger. It has made a breach in the moral consciousness of the Jewish masses, it has produced a glaring contrast between the living, though unreasoning, practice and the old theory. So many biblical and rabbinical laws being flagrantly and generally violated, the question necessarily suggests itself to many, whether both Bible and Talmud have not entirely ceased to be our religious and moral guides. In place of this unthinking and, hence, blindly destructive practice, Reform Judaism enunciates a great principle, derives from the study of Israel's history a principle, which heals the breach in the moral consciousness of the people by drawing a line of distinction between the moral laws and the ceremonial laws of Israel's religion. Its moral laws are indestructible and universal, binding on all ages and all people. Not one jot nor one tittle of them shall pass away as long as the heavens endure. But the ceremonial laws, biblical and rabbinical, have been and are merely educational means to serve ultimate moral ends. They are timely and full of value only as long as they fit in with the general conditions of society. As long as they are quick with life and purpose they are beautiful symbolic rites, helpful and healthful aids to the working of the religious ideals. But when they have lost all rational meaning and become mere fossilized forms, they are mere dead-weight, obstructing the path of true religion and clogging the spiritual progress of the soul.

Are we advocating the abolition of all religious ceremonies and rites of biblical and post-biblical origin? Heaven forbid! There are symbols which are still pregnant with beautiful significance, there are rites which tend to elevate and sanctify our lives, there are ceremonies which keep green the memories of epoch-making events in Israel's history, connecting by means of living links the past with the present. To abolish these would be like cutting away living and fruit-bearing branches from the tree of Judaism. Do we insist, in a spirit of reforming fanaticism, that all rites and ceremonies, which no longer exert an elevating and moralizing influence, should *at once* be done away with, even if they happen to be dear to the people's heart from force of hereditary habit and historical association? As long as they are no hindrance to moral progress let us leave to the slow but sure action of time to dissolve them. When they will disappear, as disappear they must for want of spiritual forces to vitalize them, the indestructible essence of religion will nowise be affected, if but the truth be firmly established in the people's heart that the moral laws alone are imperishable, while all ceremonies are transient in their nature.

This essay was originally published in slightly different form in January 1894.

CHAPTER 5

Ethnic Fictions

SOME time ago an officer in the Austrian army called a Jewish physician "an impudent Semite." The latter retorted and called the officer "an arrogant Aryan." A bloody duel was the outcome of the altercation. The two people slashed each other to vindicate the honor of their respective race. If there be evil powers that hover between heaven and earth, watching the doings of mortals, and rejoicing in their follies and crimes, they must have taken a fiendish delight in the sight of Jew and Gentile driven by the figment of an Aryan and a Semitic race to spill each other's blood. There was precious little Aryan blood in the race-proud warrior, and the doctor, though a Jew, was not much of a Semite.

There is no Aryan race anywhere in existence. And the Jews certainly can not lay claim to being pure Semites. This honor, if honor it be, belongs exclusively to the Bedouins of Arabia. During the first third or half of the 1800s the imagination of certain famous linguists gave birth to the myth of a great and homogeneous Aryan race, which, with the exception of the Basques in Spain, the Magyars in Hungary, the Turks, and the Finns, comprised all the nations of Europe, the inhabitants of Northern India, of Persia, and of Armenia. Because all those nations were found to speak kindred languages, the philologians, with pardonable but unscientific rashness jumped at the conclusion that they were all of one blood, of one race, that their common ancestors one day must have lived somewhere in Asia as a united people, governed by the same laws and institutions and worshiping the same gods.

On the basis of this fiction the scholars went on building up a spurious science of a common primitive Aryan culture, of Aryan religion and mythology, of law and government, of their racial characteristics, their emotional and intellectual traits. Imaginative writers, such as Professor Max Muller, drew charming pictures of the idyllic life which their reputed Aryan ancestors, the forefathers of the Hindus, the Iranians, the Lithuanians, the Teutons, and the Slavs once upon a time led in their Central-Asian home, dwelling together almost under the same roof. Ernest Renan, with his all-knowing retrospective imagination, did most to elaborate into a consistent system the luckless legend of an Aryan race, perennially opposed in its innermost nature, in its habits of thought and modes of feeling, in its conception of nature and life, to a fictitious Semitic race, embracing the ancient Babylonians and Assyrians, the Arameans or Syrians, the Hebrews, with their kindred, the Ammonites, the Moabites, and the Edomites, the Phoenicians and the Carthaginians, all the inhabitants of Arabia, and largely also the tribes of Ethiopia. He describes the

Aryans as the most valiant, the noblest and lordliest of races, endowed by nature with a rich and creative imagination, an intellect vigorous, profound, metaphysical, rather inclined to mysticism, and possessing constructive political powers of the highest order. He but voices, though he exaggerates, the views of the other Aryomaniacs. He exalts, above all others, the stock of which he believes all the European nations to be the living representatives, he glorifies it as the earth's natural born aristocracy, and magnifies it as the imperial race of the world, destined to bear sway over all the children of humanity by the grace of its high and indestructible native qualities.

How did Renan and the whole school of which he was the most eloquent exponent, come to know, with such wonderful exactness and fullness of detail, all the emotional and artistic, all the mental, moral, and religious characteristics of the hypothetical Aryan race? By a simple process of selection and combination. He selected the finest qualities of the noblest Grecian tribes, as displayed in the season of their richest flowering and fruit-bearing, and spoke of them as inborn qualities of the whole Aryan race. He took the grandest and ripest achievements of the Hellenic genius in the fields of poetry, art, and science, and deduced from them instinctive tendencies of the imaginary Aryan race. The rare capacity of the Roman people for military and political organization, slowly developed under favorable conditions during centuries of fierce contest and growing experience, the sturdiness, the unyielding tenacity, the undaunted courage, the iron will and domineering spirit of the Roman nation, were turned by a mere sleight of hand into innate attributes of whole Aryan families. Whatsoever things good, whatsoever things true, whatsoever things beautiful and great the Italians and the Spaniards, the Dutch, the English, the French, the Germans, and the Americans have accomplished in course of many ages in war and peace, in art, poetry, philosophy, science, and commerce, were by a delusive fancy traced back to hereditary racial powers peculiar to the fancied Aryan stock. The hymns of the Rig-Veda composed by successive generations of swarthy poets on the banks of the Indus are spoken of with comical enthusiasm as the hymns of *our ancestors,* as the oldest poems of our race. The pantheistic speculations of the Indian thinkers, and the refined mysticism of Persian Sufism, are claimed no less than the ideal philosophy of Plato, the monumental system of Aristotle, the epoch-making meditations of Descartes, and Kant's revolutionary Critique of Pure Reason, as emanations of the Aryan spirit. All the greatest men of the Western world, all the kings of poetry from Homer to Shakespeare and down to Goethe, the Indian poet Kalidasa, Firdausi, the famous poet of the Persian epic, Shahnamah, the immortal masters of art from Phidias to Canova, the most renowned statesmen from Alexander and Caesar to Charlemagne and Napoleon, the most celebrated scientists from Archimedes to Newton and Darwin, were compelled to yield their best parts in order to make up the psychology of the Aryan race. A composite photograph was taken of the supreme people of India and Persia, of Hellas and Italy, of Spain and Portugal, of Holland and England, of Germany and America, of the glorious people who within the space of nearly three thousand years appeared at long intervals in the sky of humanity. This composite photograph, looking so ideal, so beautiful, was declared to be the true likeness of the

Aryan race. It was indeed ideal but absolutely unreal, the fanciful picture of a fancied race.

This imaginary superior and aristocratic race, poetic, artistic, polytheistic, philosophical, imperial by virtue of incredible instincts, finds its natural contrast and historical antagonist in another fictitious race, the so-called Semites, whom the omniscient Renan, with his usual promptness and recklessness of judgment, brands as an inferior race. The method by which the most famous linguists, with the adventurous Renan for their spokesman, managed to draw a pen-picture of the emotional, intellectual, moral, and religious nature of the Semitic race, corresponds with that adopted in delineating the character of the Aryan race, and forms one of the most discreditable chapters in the annals of modern scholarship. The monotheism of Israel, the belief in one only God, the Maker of heaven and earth, which was the result of at least a thousand years of moral and religious development, was changed by Renan, with audacious self-assurance, into a general characteristic, into a necessary mental state of the whole race, into a religious instinct peculiar to all Semites, past and present. In the opinion of Renan and his numerous followers, all the nations regarded as members of the Semitic race, because they are known to have spoken or to speak the Semitic languages, have been and are monotheists by an invincible necessity of their mental constitution. They can not help believing in one God only. Just as spiders weave their web, as bees gather honey by instinct, so were Semites compelled by the form of their mind to believe in, and to worship, only one divinity. The Semitic mind, he says, is too narrow, too unimaginative, to believe in more than one God, to conceive of more than one divine power ruling all the phenomena of nature. The expansive imagination and creative intelligence of the Aryan race could not rest content in so narrow a faith, so beggarly an idea of the supreme power. They peopled the universe with a host of self-conscious, self-determined divinities. Every natural phenomenon was personified, and represented as a divine individual. Even after the Aryans of Europe had been converted, by persuasion or force, to a Semitic religion, the indestructible tendencies of their polytheistic soul speedily turned the barren Semitic idea of an absolute divine unity into the richer and profounder idea of a divine trinity. The belief in only one God is good enough and natural enough for the inferior Semites. But as to the Aryans, heaven forbid, that they should be satisfied with one only God ruling in the heavens above and on the earth beneath! However hard History tried, it could not change the immutable nature either of the Aryan or of the Semite. The two races are like opposite poles. Some sort of polytheism is in the blood, the feelings, and the intellect of the Aryan, while monotheism, uncompromising, fanatical, poor in ideal contents, is bound up with the very nature of the Semite.

The chain of reasoning by which Renan and other Aryomaniacs arrived at this startling generalization is as plain as it is delusive, as simple as it is false. Israel glories in the fact that it has given the religion of monotheism to the world. But did not the people of Israel belong to the inferior Semitic race? How should the spirit of originality in this one particular field, in the province of religion, have departed from the great creative race, the standard-bearer of civilization and progress, the chosen Aryan race, and come to manifest itself in so signal a manner in the midst of the Semitic Hebrews? Does it not seem like a perversion of the laws of nature and history? Starting from such false premises, only one answer could be given by thinkers who believe in blood, instinct, race, inherited tendencies, as the cause of causes, as an all-sufficient explanation of all things animate, of all things human. The Semite Israelites were believers in one God only, because they were Semites. All Semites are born monotheists, just as it is the nature of sheep to grow wool and bleat. The syllogism is perfect. The Hebrews were Semites; hence, all Semites were monotheists. You ask for proofs? Proofs shall be forthcoming. Are not the Semitic Arabs monotheists? Is not the Semitic East monotheistic? On the other hand, the whole Aryan Occident, all Europe, is Christian, Trinitarian. Is this not convincing evidence? What if History protests against such an unwarranted assumption, and is indignant at such a willful perversion of the facts, at such reckless falsification of the records? What if every page of history bears witness to the fact, that the so-called Semitic nations, Babylonians and Assyrians, the Syrians, the Phoenicians, and the rest of the Canaanites, and the Arabs down to Mohammed's time, were steeped in idolatry the most abominable, believed in innumerable gods, male and female, in gods of heaven and gods of earth, gods of the seas and of the rivers, in mountain gods and forest gods, divinities of the sun, divinities of the moon, divinities of the stars, divine rulers of life and of death and the underworld? What if proofs indisputable go to show that the Israelites themselves had for ages been rank polytheists, that there had been as many gods in Israel as there were cities in the land, that it required a thousand years of prophetic preaching, nay, that the nation as such had to be destroyed, before the leaven of paganism was overcome, and a small remnant was thoroughly and permanently converted to the belief in one God)? If the facts contradict, down with the facts! Let them perish in order that the theory of Aryan superiority and Semitic inferiority may live and prosper.

The Semites are all born monotheists, instinctive worshipers of one God. This is the first, though far from praiseworthy, characteristic of the race! Moreover, the despots of Babylonia and Assyria are known to have been fierce and cruel conquerors. There are to be seen on the ancient monuments harrowing scenes representing acts of cruelty done by the ruthless victors upon the vanquished. King David treated the conquered inhabitants of Rabbath Ammon in a manner which, to our refined humanity, must appear exceedingly inhuman. What inference was drawn from these facts? Why, they were generalized into a race quality of the Semites, and renowned writers did not hesitate to teach, with an air of scientific infallibility, that savage cruelty toward vanquished foes was a distinguishing feature in the character of the Semitic race. And what a glaring contrast such Semitic bloodthirstiness is made to form to the gentleness and the sweet uses of humanity usually displayed by Aryans against their enemies! Several days after he had slain Patroclus in battle, Achilles, the hero of the Aryan Greeks, tied the corpse of his great foe to his chariot and dragged it, driving furiously, round and round the camp, in order to appease his wrathful and vengeful heart. Yet no one ever asserted that the savage action of the ideal Greek was characteristic of the whole Aryan race. Alexander the Great destroyed the glorious city of Corinth, one of the centers of Hellenic civilization, and sold all its inhabitants into slavery. Yet no writer ever held that in so doing Alexander simply acted in obedience to the ferocious instincts of the Aryan race. Great Caesar one day ordered a whole German people, some sixty thousand persons, to be massacred in cold blood, sparing neither age nor sex. That fearful butchery is declared by historians to have been dictated by motives of far-seeing policy. But the Aryan race is not dragged in to stand godparent to it. Was it by virtue of his brutal Aryan nature that Titus caused over a hundred thousand Jewish warriors to fight with wild beasts in the arena?

Hadrian hunting the conquered Jews of Cyprus and other lands like wild beasts, is not declared by historians to have acted out of the inhuman disposition of his whole race. Historians have diverse kinds of judgment for what they regard as the Aryan and for what they designate as the Semitic race. Urged and favored by their geographical position, the ancient Phoenicians were enterprising and shrewd merchants; ages of remorseless exclusion and restriction have compelled the Jews after their dispersion to eke out a livelihood by trade. What follows? Why, the Semites of all lands and all times are born traders and money-getters. The Babylonians and the Canaanites are known to have been lascivious in their religious practices and sensual in their private conduct. Forthwith the conclusion was reached, that the whole Semitic race was and is exceedingly sensual by nature. The peculiar characteristics of the Bedouin tribes of Arabia have been worked as a rich mine of adjectives, to be applied indiscriminately to all the peoples speaking Semitic tongues. The Bedouin is avaricious and rapacious, both a miser and a spendthrift according to their varying moods. So are all the Semites. The Bedouin are unscrupulous in their dealings, lacking in truthfulness, unreliable; faithful to their guests as long as they are in their tent, treacherous as soon as they have left it. In all these respects the modern Bedouin is declared to be the typical Semite. The Bedouin is in the usual demeanor calm and dignified, but when aroused, capable of the wildest outbursts of uncontrollable passion. The Bedouin is revengeful and cruel. Lo and behold, they cry, the true son of Shem! The Bedouin dislike physical labor, and wish to earn their bread with as little muscular exertion as possible. They are of migratory habits. They are superstitious, fanatical, their religion is mainly one of fear. In all these points the Bedouin held up as the true representative of the Semitic race. In this curious way there has been formed a complete, but most incongruous, picture of the Semites.

What a strange animal the hypothetical Semite is made to be! What incredible creatures they are, made up of irreconcilable contradictions! They are moved, by the invisible wires of instinct, to utter forth with a prophet's tongue the deepest truths regarding God and the moral dignity of humanity, such as the wisest of the wise among the Aryans did not dream of, and at the same time they adore vile and vicious gods and pay homage to them in ways unmentionably abominable. They preach the gospel of love and mercy, of universal commonwealth and broadest humanity in Jerusalem, and in Babylon and Tyre they are bloodthirsty despots. In a word, the Bedouin is all things to all people and all times. Yet they do not act out their part in the free play of spontaneous development, in harmony with their changing surroundings, but they are compelled to be what they are, and to do whatever they do, by the fatality of their immutable racial nature! Through all times and all lands they form, by the indestructible laws of their being, an enduring contrast to the Aryan. They have met in thousands of places and times, they have exchanged innumerable services, they have adopted from each other the arts of civilization and learned each other's wisdom of life. But they have never blended. There is a natural gulf of separation between them. There is a deep-seated mutual antipathy between the Aryan and the Semitic races!

Many scholars have sinned grievously against the holy spirit of history and humanity by giving expression to such perverted and mischievous views. But it was chiefly the witchcraft of Renan's marvelous powers as a writer that gave currency to those pernicious theories of race, and made them popular throughout Europe and America with the educated and half-educated, from whom they gradually percolated down to the masses. Without knowing it, without willing it, Renan was in a sense the intellectual father of modern anti-Semitism. He with others sowed the poisonous seed of the baleful theory regarding the Semitic race and its eternal antagonism to the Aryan race, from which in course of a few decades the upas-tree of anti-Semitism has grown, to their own dismay and disgust. The very term anti-Semitism bears the birthmark of its origin in the laborious efforts of philosophizers. Linguists and historians gave birth to the idea of Semitism; knavish or insane agitators tacked on to it their malignant "anti." Strange fate and nemesis that Renan, the gentlest and sweetest-tempered of men, as true a lover of his kind as ever lived, should have fathered a theory, the practical consequence of which became the shame and curse of our century! Like many wise people before him, he did not give heed to his words, and did not calculate the effect which his theory might have on natures in which the instinct and the ideas of the savage lay dormant, and which only required the right word to be awakened to full life. With savages blood kinship is everything. Right and wrong, love and hate, are derived exclusively from the bonds of race. For thousands of years the prophets of Israel and their disciples have tried to substitute the moral dignity of humanity and the commonwealth of all people for the brutal conception of descent and race. Barely had these supreme ideas of humanity begun to make a deeper impression and to translate themselves into a humanizing practice, when leading scholars came up with their theories of an Aryan race and a Semitic race, drawing hard and fast lines of separation between these two races, and tracing all the grandest achievements of the human mind back to racial qualities, to hereditary instincts and tendencies. The fanaticism of nationalism in our days and the still fiercer fanaticism of race is largely due to the influence of such teachings. Since the Jews are Semites and we are Aryans, the anti-Semites say, and since Semites and Aryans are forever separated from one another by their physical and also by their moral and emotional constitution, the Jews are and forever will remain strangers in our midst, aliens that can not be assimilated with us. And since the Semites are an inferior race, their presence in our midst is a perpetual danger to our higher Aryan life and character. Fortunately, a deeper and more conscientious research, a science based on fact and not on fancies, during the last ten or fifteen years has begun to deal staggering blows to the ill-starred fiction of an Aryan and a Semitic race, and bids fair soon to drive it entirely from the temple of knowledge and rob it of all power to affect the views of people for evil.

Certain eminent scholars, foremost among them the distinguished French anthropologist Paul Broca, were not dazzled by the splendor of the Aryan theory, and asked themselves in sober earnestness, what evidence there was for assuming that nearly all the nations of Europe and many peoples of Asia form one vast homogeneous race. True, the nations in question do speak languages which are closely related to one another and may, in a sense, be regarded as but widely divergent dialects of one common speech. But does community of language prove community of race? There are eight million African-Americans in the United States and several more millions in the West Indies who speak English, the language of the New Englanders, the language of Gladstone and Tennyson. Will any one contend that the blood of Washington and Cromwell rolls in the veins of the South Carolina blacks? The Spaniards, the Portuguese, and the French speak Latin tongues, yet there is scarcely a trace of Roman blood in these nations. The Mexicans speak Spanish, a Latin dialect. Still, of pure Spaniards there is but a dwindling number in Mexico. The overwhelming mass of the natives are of Aztec blood. The present inhabitants of Greece are largely a Slavonic race, which in the eighth century occupied the lands and learned the speech of the Greeks. The Bulgarians speak a Slavonic language, but they belong to the Turkish race. The Arabic language is spoken today by all the Egyptians, the lineal descendants of the Hainitic pyramid builders, by the Berbers and Kabyles of Algiers, Tunis, Tripoli, and Morocco, the descendants of the ancient Libians and Mauritauians. By adopting the speech of the Bedouins they did not exchange their blood for that of the Arabs. The Arabic has killed off all the native languages of Asia Minor, of Mesopotamia, Syria, and Palestine. But in their racial features the populations of those countries have continued substantially what they were before the Arab conqueror had set foot there. The speech of Tunis has been in turn Numidian, Phoenician, Latin, Vandal, and Arabic. The inhabitants of southern Germany speak German; but, taken as a whole, they belong to the Celtic stock. They exchanged their Celtic speech for German within historic times. Instances too numerous to mention could be adduced from every part of the inhabited earth to prove that, under certain conditions, there is a tendency in language to spread from people to people. Spanish, Portuguese, French, German, Arabic, and, above all, English, are steadily invading new territories, occupied by races physically and mentally the most varied.

Such causes as conquest, slavery, the necessities of commercial intercourse, and religious propaganda cooperate to give to certain languages dominion over vast areas and over multitudinous tribes of people wholly unrelated to the people whose speech they have come to adopt. What has taken place within historical times, what is happening before our very eyes, doubtless, under the operation of the same causes, was going on in prehistoric ages. One such universal language, split up into numerous branches, is the Aryan speech, which is spoken by about six hundred millions of human beings through the length and breadth of Europe, in northern India and all Persian lands, in the south of Africa, and in the two Americas and Australia. Many, many thousand years ago, in the dim past of humanity, it originated somewhere in

Europe, but not in Asia, in the midst of a people which scholars are agreed to call the Aryans. It must have been a masterful people, since, like the English, the Spaniards, and the Arabs of these latter centuries, they imparted their own speech, be it by conquest or by the powers and arts of a higher civilization, to the various distinct races which inhabited and still inhabit Europe. Which of the modern European nations may be regarded as the descendants of the original and true Aryans? Most probably none. The original Aryans very likely mingled and blended with the conquered alien stocks, and, disappearing as a distinct race, left only their language behind them as the record of their power and far-reaching influence.

The fiction of an Anglo-Saxon race is one of those delusions which the pride of the English and the American hugs to its heart. They speak with unbearable vanity of the noble, glorious, invincible, creative, liberty-loving Anglo-Saxon race on both sides of the Atlantic. In listening to the Fourth-of-July spread-eagle eloquence on the Anglo-Saxon race, one would imagine that every American and every English person had nothing but the purest blood of the purest-blooded Anglo-Saxon invaders in their veins. But in reality the present Americans are a mixture of all the European races. And even the English and their purest descendants in America have at best but a streak of Anglo-Saxon blood to boast of. Only a number of noble families in England may lay claim to being largely the offspring of the invading Anglo-Saxons. But the English as a mass are Celts and Iberians. For even the Danes, who settled in certain parts of England, are like the Danes of Denmark itself, no Teutons, no genuine Scandinavians, but Teutonized Celts. The Celtic race inhabited, as Gauls and Celts, large provinces of France. T he French people thus consists of a mixture of Iberians, Ligurians, and Celts, with a sprinkling of Teutons. The present Spanish people is composed of Iberians and Celts, and in a measure, also, of Phoenicians and Jews. The south of Germany as far north as the Teutoburger Wald, the Thiiringer Wald, and the Riesengebirge is in the main Celtic in race, though German in speech. The Swiss people, whose ancestors erected pile dwellings around the Swiss lakes, belong, together with the people of northern Italy, to the same Celtic race, with a large mixture of Etruscan and other blood. The southern Italians are of quite a different race. All the nations of Slavic speech, except the Great Russians, or the Russians proper, are members of the same far-spreading race. Yet let not the Celts of France and England believe and boast that they represent the genuine high-born Aryan race. For the despised tribes of Siberia, the barbarous Finno-Tartaric tribes, that speak Turkish languages, belong to the same aristocratic race.

All of the foregoing details will suffice to convince the most skeptical mind that the belief in a close racial kinship between all the Aryan-speaking nations is a mere fiction refuted by incontrovertible facts. There exists an Aryan language, but no Aryan race. And as the fiction of an Aryan race has in the light of careful inquiry vanished like a mist, so has the myth of a Semitic race recently been condemned by the spirit of true knowledge and made to pass into the limbo of exploded delusions. Eight nations, the Babylonians, the Assyrians, the Hebrews, the southern Arabs or Sabseans, the Phoenicians, the Armenians, the Abyssinians, and the Arabs proper, are known to have spoken or still to speak languages so closely related that they may be regarded as merely dialects of one language. In their vocabulary, in their grammatical structure, and above all in the law that every root must consist of three consonants, they form among themselves the most intimate unity and stand in striking contrast to all other languages. From the community of speech the deduction has been made that all the abovementioned nations belonged to the same race, the Semitic race. But the facts brought out by the most searching investigations of the foremost anthropologists of our time flatly contradicts this assumption. Sixty thousand heads or skulls belonging to those various nations have been examined with circle and tape-measure, and the result has been "not unity of race, but a bewildering variety of racial characteristics." Only the Bedouins of Arabia form a surprising exception. They alone can be regarded as a physically homogeneous race, among whom the variations are reduced almost to a minimum. Just as their speech, though in a literary sense two thousand years younger than Babylonia, has, with wonderful tenacity, preserved the oldest and fullest forms of the original Semitic languages, so do they in their physical qualities represent the genuine Semitic race in almost absolute purity. This goes to prove that the Bedouins of today are the lineal and unmodified descendants of the primitive inhabitants of Arabia.

We only wish to call attention to the fact that they who pride themselves on being Aryans did not receive a charter from nature to be exclusive standard-bearers of civilization and the privileged creators of the arts and the wisdom of a higher life. At the same time we desire to point to the fact that we Jews are after all, by the ties of blood, second or third cousins to the very people who, as Aryans, regard us as Semitic aliens.

The result of the foregoing discussion is: The so-called Aryans consist of four distinct races; the Semites do by no means form a racial unit, and, lastly, we Jews are far from being a pure race. On the contrary, we are a very mixed race. Three elements have entered into the composition of the Jewish people: the true Semitic race, the blue-eyed, or, if you choose, the Aryan Amorites, and the Hittites, have mixed their blood to produce the Jewish or Israelitish people. The Aryan Amorites and the Armenian Hittites were turned into Israelites, into worshipers of Yahweh and followers of Moses, by a small but masterful Semitic tribe, the Bene Israel. Many a Jew will doubtless groan in spirit or be filled with indignation on being told that he shall no longer vaingloriously boast of being a member of the purest race on earth! "What are we then," many of these race-Jews will cry, "if we are not unmixed and lineal descendants of one of the tribes of Israel? Alack the day! We are told by a teacher of the religion of Israel that we are not pure Israelites. All our glory will depart from us, and the faith of the prophets will lose its hold on the Jews, if they should come to think that we are after all a very mixed race, if we can not all lay claim to being lineal descendants of those that went forth from Egypt."

To this lament of race-Jews, I reply: Let the voice of your ignorance and irreligion be hushed! There has never been a great people on earth that was of an unmixed race. Only among savages do you find pure races. The English, French, and German nations, on whose shoulders rest the civilization of Europe, have been composed out of four distinct races at least. The valiant, free, rich, and progressive American people is the most mixed of all peoples. There is hardly a race on earth that has not contributed some of its blood toward the making of this youngest nation. All the greatest nations known to history: the civilizers of the world, the Hellenes; the conquerors of the world, the Romans; the Egyptians, before whose stupendous works we stand in speechless wonder; the Babylonians and the Assyrians, who gave to the world the art of writing, of architecture, and sculpture, the science of astronomy and the elements of mathematics—all grew out of an amalgamation of various races. And should the people of Israel, that has given to the world something more precious than all the gifts bestowed by all other nations, namely, the belief in the one only God, the Maker of heaven and earth, and the Parent of all people, the belief in Yahweh, the righteous and merciful, that has given birth to the Bible, and enriched the families of the earth with the highest spiritual treasures, should that people alone have formed an exception to the universal rule and done its life-work as a pure race? All the civilized nations of the earth were welded together into a living unity by spiritual forces.

The Israelites were, closely considered, no people in the narrow and accepted sense. They were from the very beginning a religious community. It was the supreme genius of one man, of Moses, that delivered a few small Semitic tribes and a multitude of non-Semitic people from the bondage of Egypt. It was through him that the infinite mystery of all manifested itself for the first time as Yahweh, the just God, who loves the stranger, pities the oppressed, and wreaks vengeance on the cruel oppressor. For the first time in history oppression exercised in the name of race and nationality, were resisted and overcome in the name of human rights, defended by a God that loves right and hates wrong. It was on Mount Sinai that the hero of justice promulgated the leading principles of social and individual morality as a revelation of the Deity. It was there that Moses made a covenant between Yahweh and the freed people, not as between a tribe and its divinity, but as between the redeemed ones and their Redeemer, between a God of righteousness and the people that was to walk in the ways of Justice. With this step taken by Moses, the spirit of humanity broke through the bounds of race and made the attempt to establish a commonwealth on the foundation of human rights as laid down and made sacred and inviolable by the will of Yahweh. The people of Israel, as fashioned and inspired by Moses, had in itself a spiritual power of attraction and assimilation. No race and no class could be excluded from a community which had for its animating and unifying principle the belief in Yahweh, the Protector of the weak and oppressed and the Lover of right. As the Israelites marched through the wilderness they attached to themselves a number of Midianite tribes. Though by no means a numerous people, they conquered Canaan and made it the land of Israel and of Yahweh, not so much by the prowess of their arms, as by the spiritual power inherent in their religion. The seven nations were not annihilated, as a late legend would make us believe, but were assimilated by the Israelite spirit and incorporated into the people of Yahweh. Translated to Babylonia, the Jews converted the population of whole provinces to Yahvism and incorporated them into the body of the Jewish people. Only about fifty thousand Jews returned from the Babylonian captivity. But in spite of the vehement protests of the puritan nationalists against intermarriage, nearly all the pagan inhabitants of Palestine were transformed into Yahweh-worshiping

Israelites. In every province and city of the Roman Empire numerous Gentiles embraced the faith of Israel and formed nourishing congregations. And the blood of these Gentiles still rolls in our veins. In a modified form as Trinitarian Christianity, the religious spirit of Israel has conquered and assimilated the best part of humanity and made it Israelitish. But Yahvism, pure and simple, did not cease to gain accessions. The blood of the converted Turanian Khazaars has mixed with the blood of the Russian Jews. Teutonic, Celtic, Slavic, and Latin are elements that have entered into our composition. The very vigor and vitality, physical and mental, of the Jews is, next to the perennially active influences of their moralizing religion, due to the fact that they are an extremely mixed race.

Some of those who hear, and many more who will read, this lecture, will exclaim: "If we are not Jews by race, if we are not Jews by the sacred and indissoluble ties of blood, why should we continue to be Jews, why should we hold to Judaism?" To such we answer: "If you are not Jews by faith, but by race, the sooner you will depart from us, the better it will be for you, the better it will be for the mission of Yahweh, for the religion of Moses and the prophets, the religion of the psalmists and sages who worked and prayed, who lived and died not to glorify a race but to glorify the God of humanity. If I knew that there is not a drop of Semitic, not a drop of Jewish blood in my veins, I would yet cling with every fiber of my being, as long as there was breath in me, to the religious community of Israel, to the Church of Yahvism, to the monotheistic faith of pure humanity."

Abraham is not our father, Isaac did not beget us, Jacob we know not, but Yahweh, the Maker of heaven and earth, the Parent of all people, the Parent of justice and mercy, Yahweh is our Parent and our God, Yahweh is the Redeemer and Guide of spiritual and universal Israel from generation to generation.

This essay is an abridged version of the essay originally published in slightly different form as "Ethnological Fictions" in September 1898.

CHAPTER 6

Why I Am a Jew

THE very fact that the question, why I am a Jew, can be put at all, conclusively proves that to be a Jew, in the deepest sense of the word, does not mean to belong to the alleged Jewish race or nationality, but to be a member of the Jewish church. For it would be considered sheer madness, say, for a French or Spanish person to rise and explain why they are no longer French or Spanish. Once a French person, always a French person; one born of Spanish parents forever remains a Spaniard by the indestructible law of his physical identity. But one may change religion and go over from one church to another. A Buddhist may become a Christian; a Christian may embrace Islam or be converted to Judaism or to any other religion. By changing one's faith the English person does not break away from their English nationality or from their assumed Anglo-Saxon race. In asking me why I am a Jew, you do consciously or unconsciously imply that I am a Jew of my own free will and accord, and that I might choose not to be a Jew if I had a mind to. The fact is, the moment a Jew embraces Christianity, or any other religion, they cease to all intents and purposes to be a Jew. Their own father and mother no longer regard them as a Jew, though they continue to love them as a child and to respect them as a person.

The question is, therefore, perfectly pertinent. Why am I a Jew? Why do I not embrace Christianity, the religion of the leading nations of the earth, the religion of the most powerful, the most civilized and progressive portion of humanity? Why do I cling to Yahvism, the faith of the powerless, ever-struggling minority? Why do I hold fast to the religion of the Jews, who are disfranchised and persecuted in many Christian lands and regarded with inveterate prejudice and not a little contempt almost everywhere? If I were to join with my family any Christian church, it surely would not be to our worldly disadvantage. We would be received with open arms. The Christian pulpits would ring with hosannas and praises. All social barriers would fall as if by magic. We, too, would belong to the proud and powerful majority. I, too, might speak with unctuous pity of the deadening legalism of Judaism, with infinite self-satisfaction haul the Pharisees over the coals, and with upturned eyes pray to God to open the ears of the deaf Jews to the message of the cross. I, too, might in the pulpit and in my writings descant with swelling pride on our Christian civilization, expatiate on the infinite superiority of the ethics and ideals of Christianity, call and claim as Christian everything that is true, good, and beautiful in the life of humanity, and identify my little self with the greatest spiritual power in the world. Yet I forego, of my own deliberate choice, all these advantages and prerogatives and continue to be a faithful Jew. For what cogent reasons, then, am I a Jew?

First of all, I am a Jew because I believe in one only God, because I believe in the absolute and indivisible unity of the Supreme Being. I can not, by any effort of thought, imagination, or will, bring myself to believe in the Trinity, the Father, the Christ-Child, and the Holy Ghost; I can not embrace Christianity because the idea of a Triune God, of three persons in one and one in three, simply staggers my intelligence. It is as little comprehensible to me as the wildest dreams of one delirious with fever or the coruscations of a mind smitten with madness. I certainly mean no offense to my Trinitarian fellows, whose intellectual powers are as sane and strong as those of the Jews. Those impregnated from their early childhood with the dogmas of Trinitarian Christianity, no doubt, experience little difficulty in believing that the assumed three Divine Persons form an absolute unity. The human mind is wonderfully and fearfully made. It will continue to harbor through the years of intellectual maturity irreconcilable contradictions, absolutely antagonistic beliefs, if they are but implanted in the soul before the logical faculties have fully developed and become dominant, and before the intelligence has begun rigorously to apply the categories of reason to all given ideas. When such a mind emerges from the early state of passive receptivity, it finds the belief in the Trinity deeply inwrought in its very constitution, almost indissolubly interwoven with all moral ideas and ideals, intertwined with the sweet hopes of immortality, blended with the noblest spiritual aspirations. Then a fierce struggle begins in most Christian souls between faith and reason. Only a comparatively small number comes to end the inner struggle by dissolving the associations of ideas between the belief in the Triune God and all the elements of religion and ethics. It is with a bleeding heart that they break away from the cherished belief of the church, hallowed by innumerable tender memories of childhood and home. But the vast majority of Christians wrestle on bravely, and at last come forth victorious over all perplexing doubts. They find rest in the teachings of Christian apologetics that the dogma of the Trinity, though the highest truth, is yet an unfathomable and insoluble mystery, which the soul must accept with unquestioning faith. What person is infallible? Maybe the belief that three persons make up the Divine unity is a supreme transcendental truth. But we Jews are absolutely unable to give it lodgment in our mind. Were I seriously to strive to believe in a Triune God, it would wreck my mind and land me in a madhouse. If the Jews could bring themselves to believe in the Holy Trinity and in the other dogmas flowing from that central Christian belief, all would be well with them. There would be an end to the agony of ages, an end to the martyrdom of body and soul, an end to calumny and isolation. By suffering baptism, we would dive down into the stream of the nations, the waves would swallow up our identity, Israel would be but a name and a memory.

As the deer longs after water brooks, so does the soul of the Jew long after peace and union. But we will not purchase peace and union at the price of humanity's dearest possession, at the price of prophetic universal monotheism, without tinge and taint. Our souls are chained by ties unbreakable to the fiery chariot of ethical, historical monotheism. We must go with it, though it lead us through the valley of

the shadow of death and the world's contempt. The
will of Yahweh compels us to proclaim, "Hear, O
Israel, the Eternal, our God, the Eternal is One." The
power of Yahweh is upon us, fastening upon our
conscience and mind the mission of monotheism which
we can not shake off. The word of Yahweh is in us
strong as death, and we must obey it, even to our hurt.
We still hear the voice of God's prophet: "Ye are my
witnesses that I am God, I am the Eternal, and beside
Me there is no Savior. Ye are my witnesses that I am
God, and beside Me there is none else." Not simply
for our sake, but for the sake of the world, and in
particular of the Christian world, do we hold fast to the
mission of being witnesses to the absolute unity of
God. Trinitarian Christianity is ever in danger of
degenerating unconsciously into polytheism. To
realize the three distinct Divine Persons as one Being
is a tremendous strain on the Christian mind. The
intelligence, under the sway of the logical categories,
is constantly tried to break up in consciousness the
Triune God into a triad of divinities, whereby
Christianity would cease to be a monotheistic religion.
The religion of Israel, the ever present church of
Yahweh, serves the Christians as a warning against the
insidious polytheistic tendency, and stimulates the
Christian mind to lay the utmost emphasis on the unity
of God. Without the Jew, who is the living witness of
uncompromising monotheism, the Christians would be
less on their guard against the danger lurking in the
dogma of the Trinity, and might, as in the darkest days
of the Middle Ages, drift more and more in the
direction of polytheism. For rendering them this
service the Christians owe gratitude to the Jews.

I am a Jew because I can not accept the Christian
scheme of salvation and incarnation; my soul shrinks

from it in dread and awe. The idea of God, the absolute and infinite, assuming the flesh and form of a person, being a babe at His mother's breast, passing through the stage of childhood, growing to the stature of adulthood, eating, drinking, fasting, thirsting, sleeping, weeping and laughing like a person, the idea of God Almighty being scourged, nailed to the cross, and dying like a mortal, is not only unthinkable, unimaginable, and unbelievable to me, but a denial of what is to Israelites the very essence of religion. God is not a person or the son of a person. God is not born of woman nor does God suffer and die like a mortal. I know there are myriads of Christians who are wiser and better than I, to whom the incarnation is the be-all of their faith, the beginning, middle, and end of their theology. But it is just because I can not believe with them in the mystery of the incarnation that I am a Jew.

I am a Jew because I do not and can not believe in the Christian dogma of the fall of humanity, of original sin, of vicarious atonement, of redemption through the blood of Jesus. I do not believe that the human race fell through the alleged sin of Adam from the state of moral perfection and blessedness. The story of the Bible merely states in a mythical form that there existed neither physical nor moral good and evil as long as the mind of humanity was in the state of happy, because ignorant, infancy. I am a Jew because for the life of me I can not believe that an all-good and all-just God decreed that the sin of the first two people, if sin it was, should descend as a moral blight and inextinguishable curse to all their descendants. I am a Jew because the idea is abhorrent to me that the all-merciful God found no other way to appease unrighteous anger save by means of a great sacrifice, by the sacrifice of the God-man, the child of God, the

110

second person in the Trinity. To my benighted Jewish mind this dogma appears a ghastly travesty on the idea of divine justice and mercy. Yet among those who hold this belief are godly and holy people whose shoe-strings I am unworthy of loosening. Maybe their theory of divine government is true. But I can not worship such a God. I would rather walk in the darkness of unbelief. I would rather be crushed by God's power for rebelling than bend my knee to a God whom I can not adore as just and merciful.

I am a Jew because I can not believe in the miraculous power of Jesus, be he a human or a God, to redeem people from the evils of ancestral sins and from the effects of their own guilt. I believe in atonement through repentance, through change of heart and conduct. But vicarious atonement is to my mind mere religious magic. I wish I could indulge in such pleasant hopes. It is an easy way of getting rid of sins by letting the sufferings of Jesus atone for them. But I can not entertain such a belief. I am responsible to my conscience and my God for my sins. No mediator stands between my soul and my Maker, to obtain pardon for me through their influence and merit. Face to face I stand with the majesty of my Judge and Lawgiver, and between God and me there is no other Savior. I bear the burden of my sins and accept the consequences thereof, I hear God's warning and judging voice in my conscience, and God's mercy is revealed in the thousand responses of my heart. I am a Jew because I can not believe in the strangest of all miracles that the wine and the bread taken at the communion table are turned in the worshiper into the blood and the flesh of Jesus. This dogma is authoritatively taught by the Catholic Church as well as by some Protestant churches. I am a Jew because I

can not believe with the Christians that there is no
salvation for those who deny Jesus, who have no faith
in the atoning power of his blood and death. I am a
Jew because I do not believe that salvation here and
hereafter depends on baptism in the name of Jesus
Christ. I am a Jew because I believe that the righteous
live by their own faith, justice, and mercy, and the
wicked perish through their own moral degradation
and sin.

Many will doubtless say: "Why, you are identifying
Christianity with exploded dogmas in which few
educated people really believe in our day. They are
officially and perfunctorily paraded in articles of
creed, in order not to break up the historical continuity
of Christianity. The Christian religion does not consist
in the dogmas of the trinity, the divinity of Jesus, the
incarnation, the resurrection, and vicarious atonement.
These dogmas are but the historical trappings and
temporary symbols in which the Christian idea has
inadequately expressed itself. The abiding essence of
Christianity consists in the ideal character and life of
Jesus and his sublime ethical teaching." To this I
make bold to reply: Christianity without the trinity,
without the divinity of Jesus, without the incarnation
and vicarious atonement, Christianity stripped of all
its distinctive characteristics, is nothing but the
universal religion of Yahweh, such as was conceived
and proclaimed by the greatest prophets and wisest
teachers of Israel, among whom I count and reverence
the immortal prophet and teacher of Nazareth.
Christianity without a Christian dogma is not the
religion of the genuine historical Christian churches.
It is the universal faith which is usually named
Judaism. It is what I call Yahvism in order to
dissociate it in consciousness from the element of the

race. It is the universal religion of broad humanity, of justice, of love and holiness. It is the religion of Moses, of Amos, Isaiah, Jeremiah, Hillel, and Jesus. It is the ethical monotheism of Israel without the limitations and the trammels of race, without the yoke of ceremonial law. It is the religion which I and all enlightened rabbis profess and teach.

But do not the new moral ideas and ideals of Jesus, without the dogmas of the incarnation, the resurrection, and vicarious atonement, constitute an essentially new religion, distinct from Yahvism, superior to it in every respect? By no means, I answer. The teachings of Jesus are absolutely identical in their general principles, as well as in their special applications, with those of the Old Testament and the Talmud. There is no moral idea, no moral ideal, in the New Testament which is not inculcated with all possible emphasis, and proclaimed with glowing enthusiasm, in the Old Testament and the Talmud. There is not a moral saying of Jesus, no ethical truth preached by him, that we Israelites do not accept with all our heart and all our soul, and try to live up to. There is no doubt with us that the ethical teaching of Jesus is nothing but the quintessence of the highest biblical ethics and the finest essence of the still more highly-developed morality of the post-biblical masters, presented with sublime pathos and heart-bewitching power by a great soul. There is no new revelation to us Israelites in the Sermon on the Mount, no step is made therein beyond the prophets' lofty ideals of love, charity, humility, and piety as taught by the rabbis, the predecessors and contemporaries of Jesus. But the Sermon on the Mount is a glorious summary and incomparable presentation of the moral and religious ideas and ideals which the spirit of God, through fifteen centuries, slowly and steadily, with ever-increasing power and light, had been unfolding through the soul of Israel. And that soul of Israel, the prophetic, God-seeking, God-loving soul, which wholly consecrates itself to God by loving all God's children, by meting out to all human beings the fullest measure of justice, by pouring out the rich streams of loving-kindness unto all people without distinction of race or creed; that soul of Israel was stirring with might and dwelling with radiant beauty in the breast of the son of Joseph and Mary, and expressed itself with majestic eloquence and heart-conquering grace and simplicity in his sermons, his parables, and, above all, in his pure and holy life. We Israelites claim Jesus of Nazareth as our own, as one of our best and greatest masters, as one of our immortal fathers, as one of our saintliest heroes of righteousness and love. Whatever crimes have been committed against us by cruel and misguided people in his name, verily we do not charge him with them. Those blind and heartless fanatics did not learn cruelty from him, the teacher of love. Surely the example of the meek and lowly rabbi of Galilee, who taught with the prophets and teachers of Israel to suffer persecution and not to persecute, did not inspire the zealots with the fury and madness of persecution. We claim the ethical teachings of Jesus, as preserved in the Gospels, as our own spiritual possession.

Still, my holding Jesus in profoundest veneration, my enthusiasm for his sublime teachings, does not make me a Christian. Just as little are those Gentiles true Christians who, like me, deny his divinity and all the beliefs which cohere with that cardinal dogma. I make bold to express my humble opinion that the true Unitarian church is a section or sect of the universal church of Yahvism, within which Jesus lived, moved, and had his being, and of whose truths and ideals he was a glorious exponent. But why do I not join the Unitarians, with whom I agree in most essentials of faith and practice? My answer is: A large wing of the Unitarians still coquette with the peculiar dogmas of Christianity. There is a wonderful magic in historical words and names. They tend to draw people back to their former contents. The world still needs the ancient historical church of uncompromising prophetic monotheism. For God's sake, for humanity's sake, we can not renounce the mission of standing guard around the ark of monotheism entrusted to us by the seers and martyrs of Israel. For this reason I am a Jew, and not a Unitarian.

One more reason I shall give for being a Jew, and I shall have done: The Gentiles who have totally discarded Christianity and, to all intents and purposes, are at one with us in faith, shrink from identifying themselves with poor, despised, scattered, and maligned Israel. They are afraid of losing caste by being named together with the Jews as associates in the same church. But I am a Jew for that very reason that the Jews are in all Christian lands under the ban of social prejudice, and are in many kingdoms disfranchised and oppressed under the very shadow of the cross. I follow the example of the two great Jewish martyrs, Jeremiah and Jesus. They made their home among the poor and despised. They ate the bread of affliction with those who were sore of heart and poor in spirit. Their great souls' love belonged to the down-trodden and outcast children of God. Their companions and friends were in the hovels of poverty, not among the mighty in palaces and courts. I, too, inspired by their example and teachings, wish to be a Jew in these latter days. I cast my lot with the despised. I am a brother to the most wretched and hopeless of people, to the Russian Jews, whose faces and forms tell the woeful tale of Christian persecution and contempt killing body and soul. You, proud Christians, are amazed at the sight of the Russian Jews, so disfigured and scarcely human in visage. But I bid them welcome in their rags to my heart and home. I touch their sores with a brother's tender hand. Their bruises are my bruises; I bleed with their wounds; I quiver with the stripes, physical and moral, which poor Israel receives at the hands of Christian rulers and nations. You have a smile and a contemptuous name for the people of endless sorrows. But their sorrows sit brooding over my soul by day and night. The misery of the Jews, of whatever land, poisons my joys and makes life a martyrdom to me. The shame and dishonor with which malicious tongues try to brand them burn themselves into my soul. The demon fury which rages against the Jews in anti-Semitic Germany, Austria, and Romania haunts my waking hours and torments me in my very dreams. The blasphemous philosophy of Christian thinkers which declare the Jew to be doomed by the curse of heredity to moral inferiority, makes me blush for humanity. The contemptuous tolerance of good Christians, the exaggerated praises they bestow upon the Jew with a patronizing air, fill me with pain and loathing. I will not take refuge in a church to save myself and my children from the common lot of the Jews. I sit on the ground with my family to take their hands in mine. I strive to raise them with what power there is in me to new spiritual heights, whence they shall see the landscape of the future blooming with blessings universal, which they and their parents have sown with tears. I pray God to open their eyes that they may see the church universal of Yahweh standing as a new Jerusalem with seven gates flung wide open, through which the Gentiles may stream in to kneel with us at the altar of the righteous and merciful God of Humanity, and blend their voices with ours in the cry: "Hear, O humanity, Yahweh, our God, Yahweh is One."

This essay was originally published in slightly different form in October 1897.